Empire: A Very Short Introduction

Very Short Introductions available now:

For more information visit our web site:
www.oup.co.uk/general/vsi/

Stephen Howe

EMPIRE

A Very Short Introduction

OXFORD
UNIVERSITY PRESS

OXFORD
UNIVERSITY PRESS

Great Clarendon Street, Oxford OX2 6DP

Oxford University Press is a department of the University of Oxford.
It furthers the University's objective of excellence in research, scholarship,
and education by publishing worldwide in

Oxford New York

Auckland Bangkok Buenos Aires Cape Town Chennai
Dar es Salaam Delhi Hong Kong Istanbul Karachi Kolkata
Kuala Lumpur Madrid Melbourne Mexico City Mumbai Nairobi
São Paulo Shanghai Taipei Tokyo Toronto

Oxford is a registered trade mark of Oxford University Press
in the UK and in certain other countries

Published in the United States
by Oxford University Press Inc., New York

British Library Cataloguing in Publication Data

Data available

Library of Congress Cataloging in Publication Data

Data available

ISBN 978-0-19-280223-1

17 19 20 18 16

Typeset by RefineCatch Ltd, Bungay, Suffolk
Printed in Great Britain by
Ashford Colour Press Ltd, Gosport, Hants.

Contents

List of illustrations

The publisher and the author apologize for any errors or omissions in the above list. If contacted they will be pleased to rectify these at the earliest opportunity.

Introduction: I read the news today . . .

A great deal of the world's history is the history of empires. Indeed it could be said that *all* history is imperial – or colonial – history, if one takes a broad enough definition and goes far enough back. Since this short book is trying to say something about the entire history of humanity, from the earliest times and right around the globe, the only sensible place to start is with today's newspapers.

'Today' is a day when I am – I hope – almost finishing work on this book, 14 February 2002. In a gesture of parochialism which the rest of the book tries to avoid, I'll limit myself to the main London papers of this day; though I can also browse newspapers from all around the world as they appear, with my deplorably limited language skills as the only restriction. This is thanks to the Internet, a communication system which some, perhaps rather overexcited, critics describe as a new kind of global empire. Still, the better British papers carry stories from all round the world – and almost all of them seem, in one way or another, to involve the legacies of empires.

For many Westerners, 14 February is St Valentine's Day, when lovers exchange cards and gifts. The custom has, only very recently, become popular in India too. But, one British newspaper reported, activists of the conservative Hindu party Shiv Sena protested bitterly and aggressively against it. The celebration was, they complained, crassly materialistic and immoral. It was an alien cultural import, which had nothing to do with Indian tradition or religion, and indeed threatened them. It was outrageous that young Hindus should mark – however irreligiously – a day named after a Christian saint. The anti-Valentine zealots of Shiv Sena are not just grouching about a harmless festivity. They are, in their own eyes at least, resisting the forces of cultural imperialism. St Valentine, along with McDonalds, Coca-Cola, Western pop music, and 'loose' sexual morals, is part of a global menace to Indian civilization. Resisting that rather obscure saint's influence is a continuation of India's long anticolonial struggle.

The *Guardian*'s leading story was more sombre. It reported that the United States was planning renewed war against Saddam Hussein's Iraq, with which it had been in intermittent conflict for over a decade. Iraqis, and critics of US policy in general, routinely described its repeated threats and incursions against the Arab state as imperialist, with some alleging that the real motivation was to maintain American-owned multinational companies' control over the oil reserves of the region. From another viewpoint it was Iraq, allegedly a permanent threat to its neighbours – it had briefly conquered and annexed Kuwait in 1990–1 – which harboured aggressive, empire-building ambitions. And the very existence of Iraq and its neighbours, as well as the location of the borders between them, owed almost everything to the colonial past. They had been carved out from the ruins of the Ottoman empire by Britain and France, in the second decade of the 20th century.

Another fairly direct consequence of the Middle East's brief era of European colonial rule featured heavily in the day's papers, as it had done almost every day in recent months: violence between Israelis and Palestinians. Some, especially in the Arab world, saw Israel's very existence as a colonialist phenomenon. Others blamed Britain, the former colonial power, for its early sponsorship of the Zionist movement. But many Israelis viewed their country's emergence and survival as an *anti*colonialist story, involving struggle against both British and Arab imperialism.

In Istanbul, the linguist and veteran political campaigner Noam Chomsky – best known for his many critiques of American 'imperialism' around the globe – won a court case over Turkish government censorship of his writings on the Kurdish problem. This was in many eyes – though not in those of Turkish nationalists – yet another consequence of empire, in that Kurdish grievances in Turkey and elsewhere stemmed ultimately from their failure to achieve national self-rule when the region's old imperial system broke up in the early 20th century.

For most, though, the dominant international story was the Hague trial of former Yugoslav leader Slobodan Milošović, accused of war crimes in the Balkan turmoil of the 1990s. The conflicts in which Milošović played so deadly a role are, on the long view, legacies of the Ottoman and Austro-Hungarian empires, which ruled the region until just over 100 years ago. More immediately, the wars in Bosnia and Kosovo, for whose conduct he was being tried, were ones where every participant – from tiny Albania to the American superpower – was accused of imperialist aggression by its enemies.

The court where he was tried is, to some, also an imperialist creation. For such critics, the whole idea of 'universal' human rights is actually a gigantic fraud, where Western imperialist or ex-colonial powers try to pass off their own, very specific and localized, idea of what 'rights' should be as universal, trampling roughly over everyone else's beliefs and traditions. The very structure of 'international law' was created in the colonial era, by the colonial powers. It is based on a mixture of Napoleonic, Anglo-Saxon, and before that Roman legal codes, owing nothing much to any non-European idea of legality. But then the legal systems of most ex-colonies, too, are based on those of their former masters.

British Prime Minister Tony Blair had just returned from visiting various former British colonies in Africa. While there, he had urged that more must be done to help resolve those countries' endemic problems of poverty and unrest. The opinion pages and readers' letters columns of several newspapers carried numerous contributions to an argument – the latest of many such exchanges down the years – over how far the travails of independent Africa should be blamed on the colonial inheritance, and even whether Africa might be better off if the colonialists returned. Other correspondents, notably in the conservative *Daily Mail*, expressed outrage that British sovereignty over Gibraltar, one of its few remaining overseas dependencies, might be abridged. In Zimbabwe, as an election approached, the government accused the main opposition party of being a tool of imperialism and a threat to national independence, while it was itself alleged to be depriving white Zimbabweans – descendants of British colonial settlers – of their right to vote. The Obituary pages of the day's papers also recalled Britain's long involvement with African affairs, for Maurice Foley, a Labour politician who had been one of Westminster's most prominent 'Friends of Africa' in the 1950s and 1960s, had died.

Blair, meanwhile, was under siege from accusations that he had used undue influence to help a British-based Indian industrialist, Lakshmi Mittal, acquire Romania's previously state-owned steel factories. This too was a 'postcolonial' affair in several ways. An Indian businessman would surely not be running a British-linked company, nor making donations to a British political party, if Britain had not once ruled India. To some critics, the fact that a 'Western' company was buying up decrepit industrial plants in Romania was a manifestation of economic imperialism. To others, the fact that the Romanian steel industry *is* decrepit was the fault of another, now defunct kind of empire, the Soviet Communist one. Others again say that the British political traditions of supposedly over-centralized, unaccountable executive power which allowed Mr. Blair to act as he allegedly did, without consulting anyone else, are a legacy of the empire. According to that view, habits of autocratic rule once used to dominate 'them', colonial subjects across the globe, still afflict 'us' at home. Britain itself, some say, is the last colony of the British empire.

A Scottish parliament, exercising law-making powers that Scotland had lost 300 years before and only partly regained in 1998, voted to ban fox-hunting. Enthusiasts for that barbarous pastime – which may have come to the British Isles along with the Norman or the Roman imperial invaders, and may even derive ultimately from the habits of central Asian nomads who built vast but short-lived empires across Eurasia 1,500 years ago – were outraged. But such enthusiasts were not numerous in Scotland. Many Scots muttered that fox-hunting was basically an English 'sport' anyway, not a truly Scottish one – and England's influence over Scotland, cultural as well as political, has in their eyes always been a kind of colonialism.

A dozen stories reminded anyone who needed such reminders that migrants from Britain's former colonies featured in every aspect of British life. Court cases were in process over the murder of a Nigerian-born schoolboy, a black 'supermodel's claim that a newspaper had invaded her privacy, and the alleged terrorist activities of militant British Islamists, mostly of Pakistani family background. An Indian-born MP had to apologize to colleagues for breaches of parliamentary rules – and, seemingly irrelevantly to the issue at hand, punctuated his statement with avowals that he was proud of his ethnic origins. The fact that so many of these stories concerned crimes and misdemeanours perhaps hinted at how troubled some aspects of post-imperial Britain's multiracialism had been. But the newspapers' sports and arts pages gave a more positive, surely more balanced picture. Darius Vassell was the outstanding success in England's generally lacklustre footballing performance against Holland. Both Vassell and the England team's other 'new boy', Michael Ricketts, were the children of colonial immigrants, as were three other team members. On the other side of the world another such, Nasser Hussein, was captaining an England eleven which struggled against New Zealand in the quintessentially imperial game, cricket. The Arts section of the ultra-conservative *Daily Telegraph*, meanwhile, had as its main feature an interview with three women singers of Jamaican parentage, the vocal group Mis-Teeq, tipped as the 'Best British newcomers' in pop music.

Echoes of empire recurred on the levels of imagination and metaphor as well. The Oscar nominations were announced. Leading the field by some way was the cinematic adaptation of J. R. R. Tolkien's *Lord of the Rings*, an epic fantasy of clashing empires, exotic cultural encounters, and an evil power's drive for world domination. And a senior British policeman was quoted as saying that a disgraced colleague had run an 'empire of evil' among the local bobbies of Cleveland.

Although the great historic imperial systems – the land-based Russian one as well as the seaborne empires of Western European powers—have collapsed during the past half-century, their legacies shape almost every aspect of life on a global scale. Meanwhile there is fierce argument – and much speculation – about what has replaced the old territorial empires in world politics. Do the United States and its allies, transnational companies, financial and media institutions, or most broadly the forces of 'globalization', constitute a new imperial system? Ranging across this vast field, I shall attempt in this short book to do three, intertwined jobs:

First, an interpretation of what the 'idea of empire' has meant (in very broad terms, of course!) across the centuries and continents, to its rulers, subjects, and subsequent analysts.

Second, an essay in conceptual and historiographical clarification: trying, in not too ponderously classificatory a style, to disentangle the multiple uses and abuses of the labels 'empire', 'imperialism', 'colonialism', 'colonization', 'neo-colonialism', and so on.

Third, an 'inventory' of imperialism's diverse and often bizarre

1. A classic image of the height of Britain's imperial power: Victoria presents a Bible to an adoring native. *The Secret of England's Greatness* by Thomas Jones Barker combines themes of power, piety, royalty, the obligations of the rulers, and the abject gratitude of the ruled.

afterlives in the contemporary world: both the 'real world' of geopolitics and the various intellectual fields involved in studying or arguing about colonialism and its various 'posts'.

Chapter 1
Who's an imperialist?

The very word empire, as we shall see, has had a complicated history and many different, fiercely contested meanings. It has also been intertwined with several other, mostly newer but equally contentious words: imperialism, colonialism, and latterly neo-colonialism, globalization, and others. A great range of compound terms has also been thrown into the stew at different times and places: informal empire, sub-imperialism, cultural imperialism, internal colonialism, postcolonialism, and many more. All these labels tend to come attached to heavy luggage: a great weight of history and ideology, sometimes of elaborate theorizing, sometimes of raw emotion. To make everything just that bit more difficult still, the relationships of these various terms to one another are also all much debated, and sometimes much confused. One indicator of that might be that there has been hesitation over what the very title of this 'Very Short Introduction' should be: 'Empire', the plural 'Empires', 'Imperialism', or perhaps 'Colonialism'.

The difficulties involved are not just conceptual but political and emotional. Defining something as imperial or colonial today almost always implies hostility to it, viewing it as inherently immoral or illegitimate. If someone calls, say, American actions in Afghanistan, British policies in Northern Ireland, or Chinese ones in Tibet 'imperialist' or 'colonialist', they may or may not be alluding to some weighty theory about the causes or character of those actions. They are, though, almost certainly telling us one thing quite clearly: they very much dislike whatever it is they are talking about.

The idea that empire is a Bad Thing suffuses almost all our imaginative worlds too: in the literature of science fiction and fantasy, in popular cinema, in video and computer games. In the *Star Wars* films, the bad guys are the Evil Empire. In *The Lord of the Rings*, the wicked Sauron controls an empire and schemes to rule over all. Noble Gondor, by contrast, is a 'realm' or a kingdom – even though some analysts of Middle Earth's historical sociology would doubtless call Gondor's large, multi-ethnic political system an imperial one. Hobbits, meanwhile, live in a small republic with no monarch and indeed hardly any government at all. The oddest twist to this is that the Shire of the Hobbits is so obviously England, although when the book was written, its author's 'England' still ruled a global empire. And in J. R. R. Tolkien's youth, the mass media, popular culture, and much of the art of the day would have reflected an image of empire seemingly almost the opposite of today's. To be an empire builder was to be an adventurer, a hero, a selfless labourer for others' well-being. Such approving imagery dominated depictions not only of modern Britain but of ancient Rome. It extended far beyond the empire-owning countries, across Europe, the Atlantic and even the globe. In countries like Ireland and Poland, which not only possessed no colonies but were seen by many as the victims of others' colonialism, writers and artists were nonetheless enthralled by visions of imperial greatness. Pioneer Indian or Egyptian nationalists, Pan-Africanists, and Pan-Arabists raged against the European empires which ruled their lives. But, far more often than is usually now recalled, they were also led on by ideas that in the mists of the past, they too once had empires of their own – and might in future have them once more.

Ideas about empire have not only changed across the past century from general approval to near-universal distaste; they have also seemed to spread and multiply beyond all limit or control. 'Imperialism', as a word, has gone imperial; 'colonialism' has colonized our languages. They do not only span the galaxies and the parallel universes of science fiction. They have come to be used, at the extreme, to describe anyone's, any group's, or anything's supposed superiority, or domination, or even just influence, over any other person, or group, or thing. Some of these uses are clearly metaphorical; others seem to be intended literally. Our everyday lives are 'colonized', in a wide range of current rhetorics, by technology, by bureaucracy, or by the advertising industry. Almost any large organization in commerce, finance, media, or even sports is an 'empire' to those who dislike it. For some fans of rival British football clubs, Manchester United is 'the Evil Empire': and the label is not *entirely* a joke nor, perhaps, *only* a metaphor.

Even leaving aside such rhetorical excesses, the political uses of these words may seem quite unmanageably wide and various. The same people, at different times or according to different viewpoints, could be seen as imperialists and as victims of imperialism, as colonizers, colonized, and postcolonial. In the later 18th century, white settlers on the eastern seaboard of North America, after mostly destroying the earlier inhabitants and enslaving Africans, began to see themselves as victims of domination from England. They were colonists – and, in a slightly later language, colonialists – who also mounted the world's first successful anticolonial revolution. White Australians are clearly heirs to a colonial project of British expansion and settlement. In some eyes, they remain colonialists vis-à-vis Aboriginal Australians, who are still underprivileged, marginalized, and deprived of many of their ancestral lands. Yet many Australians see themselves, with some justice, as coming at least as much from an *anti*colonial political tradition, which struggled for and won effective independence from Britain. In so far as that struggle was successful, Australia today is – at least by some definitions of another much-disputed word – a *post*colonial society. Others again argue, though, that Australia remains tied to the remnants of British imperial power, at least in that it is not a fully sovereign Republic, but formally subject to the British Monarchy – or even because social attitudes are still

2. **Resisters:** Skeletons with battle injuries, excavated at Maiden Castle, Dorset, England. These were most likely British defenders of the Durotriges people, killed fighting against the Roman invasion in *c.*45 CE.

influenced by what a former Australian Prime Minister, Paul Keating, called a 'cultural cringe' towards the old imperial masters. To complete the circle, certain conservative Australian politicians raise the alarm that their country risks being 'colonized' by large-scale Asian immigration, or subject to a 'new imperialism' from Japanese and other Asian economic powers.

The terms 'empire' and 'imperialism', at their most general, have been used to refer to any and every type of relation between a more powerful state or society and a less powerful one. In order to arrive at a more usefully specific understanding, we need to delve a little into the histories of the words.

The word 'empire' comes, of course, from the Latin *imperium*: for which the closest modern English equivalent would perhaps be 'sovereignty', or simply 'rule'. For the Romans, it denoted a dual capacity: to wage war and to make and execute laws. An 'emperor' was originally a victorious general, later a supreme magistrate – though the military overtones of the title never disappeared. But it also came, even in later Republican Rome, to have a further connotation: size. *Imperium* came to mean rule over extensive, far-flung territories, far beyond the original 'homeland' of the rulers. As the term was taken up again in the early-modern period, by European Christian monarchs and their publicists, it usually – indeed increasingly – carried this connotation; though some rather petty rulers, like Anglo-Saxon kings in parts of England, also occasionally and vaingloriously called themselves emperors. But it carried also two further, and for some time probably more important, associations. One was of *absolute* sovereignty, acknowledging no overlord or rival claimant to power. When Henry VIII of England had his realm proclaimed an 'empire' in the 1530s, the main intention was to assert that he owed no allegiance to, and would tolerate no interference from, either the Papacy or the secular power with which it was aligned, the Habsburg domains. The other was found especially in the most explicitly religious uses of the term: an aspiration to universality. Christian empire was in principle boundless, as the Roman *imperium* to which it was partial heir had claimed to be. Everyone outside was a barbarian (an idea Rome had adapted from the Greeks).

With the advent of a universalist, Christian monotheism, the notion was added that all these outsiders were by definition not only uncivilized but ungodly. A very similar idea, though expressed of course in different language, came to be held by early Islamic rulers; while a more distantly related belief was espoused also by Chinese thinkers. Thus for such inferior peoples to be brought under the sway of universal empire by conquest would also be to bring them access to civilization and true religion – though Christians and Muslims differed on whether this meant they should be converted by force. Conquest was therefore morally justified, even divinely ordained. A new, perhaps more intense drive for expansion, peculiar to the Christian and Islamic West, was thus created. This whole complex of ideas also eventually became associated with two further notions; those of nationality and of race. The association was complex, and is much argued over, though most historians tend to see nationalism, and racialized thought, as much more modern additions to the ancient and medieval core.

Moving from early self-understandings to modern attempts at definition, these have been extremely numerous and various: some notably vague, others immensely elaborate, indeed ponderous. A kind of basic, consensus definition would be that an empire is a large political body which rules over territories outside its original borders. It has a central power or core territory – whose inhabitants usually continue to form the dominant ethnic or national group in the entire system – and an extensive periphery of dominated areas. In most cases, the periphery has been acquired by conquest. But sometimes, especially in the medieval world, expansion comes about by the intermarriage of ruling families from two previously independent states: historians have used such labels as 'composite monarchy' for the resulting units. And in some modern instances, the people of the peripheral territory may have chosen willingly to be brought under the control of the imperial centre. Nineteenth-century British governments, for example, claimed – not always honestly – that new areas coming under their control did so because their inhabitants positively begged to be protected by British power. Thus such places were not conquered colonies, but 'Protectorates'. Later, and with more justification, Britain and France argued that the scattered, mostly small overseas territories which remained under their rule in the early 21st century did so in part because the people of British Gibraltar or the Falklands islands, or French Martinique, wanted it that way.

Empires, then, must by definition be big, and they must be composite entities, formed out of previously separate units. Diversity – ethnic, national, cultural, often religious – is their essence. But in many observers' understanding, that cannot be a diversity of equals. If it is, if there is no relation of domination between 'core' and 'periphery', then the system is not an empire but deserves a title such as 'commonwealth'. So 20th-century British governments argued that they were engineering a gradual transformation from a London-dominated empire to a Commonwealth, a free association of equals. In somewhat similar fashion, the rulers both of the Soviet Union and the post-Soviet Russian federation insisted that those were not imperial systems, because all their component parts had equal rights – at least on paper.

Empires always involve a mixture of direct and indirect rule. The central power has ultimate sovereignty, and exercises some direct control, especially over military force and money-raising powers, in all parts of its domain. But there will usually be some kind of decentralized, 'colonial', or 'provincial' government in each of the empire's major parts, with subordinate but not trivial powers of its own. These authorities may be – indeed in most imperial systems, usually are – headed by men sent out from the dominant centre. But their leaders, and certainly their more junior administrators or enforcers, may also be 'locals', drawn from the ranks (often, indeed,

15

from the pre-conquest ruling orders) of the dominated people. In many empires, ancient and modern, there was a general tendency over time for imperial rulers to devolve ever more power to such groups. In the long run, of course, this might lead to the gradual breakup of the empire itself. But, as we shall see, many historians argue that the key to understanding empire lies in the bargains struck between imperial centre and local 'collaborators'. No empire could last for long if it depended entirely on naked power exerted from the centre outwards. The different kinds of collaboration – it's a word often carrying hostile overtones, especially from Second World War Europe, but will be used here in a more neutrally intended sense – will therefore be a major theme in these pages. In almost all empires, local intermediaries might enjoy much autonomy within their own spheres, and command considerable wealth, power, and status, in return for delivering their people's obedience, financial tribute, and military services to the centre.

The emphasis on intermediaries, collaborators, bargains, and decentralization should not, however, be pushed too far. Empire was also often, indeed perhaps typically, established and maintained by violence. Sometimes extreme violence: some historians would say that most episodes of genocide and mass murder in world history have been associated with empire-building. We shall explore this link below. In the modern world, the idea of empire has also usually been associated with European, white rule over non-Europeans, with 'racial' hierarchies and racist beliefs. Some analysts, again, build this association into their very definitions of empire and colonialism. But this causes some obvious problems. If neither conquerors nor conquered are 'European' – or if both are – should the resulting system be called imperial? Should we say, for instance, that the polities ruled by Ming emperors, or by Ottoman ones, were somehow not 'proper' empires? Or that they may have been empires, but their activities were not 'imperialist' or 'colonialist' because those labels are stamped 'whites only'? Not many historians feel comfortable with such manoeuvres. It is more sensible, surely, to say that the modern European colonial empires

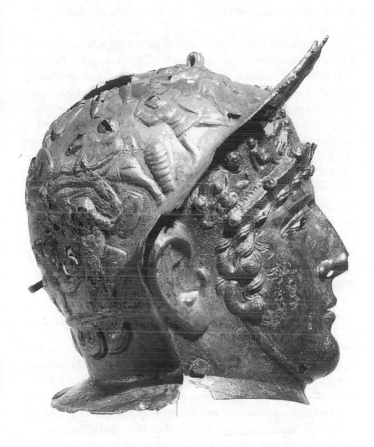

3. **Collaborators: Roman ceremonial cavalry helmet found at Ribchester, Lancashire, England, 2nd century CE.** The wearer was probably a Sarmatian Slav from the Danube basin – recruited from one of the empire's extreme peripheries, serving at its other extremity.

were special kinds of imperial system, and that ideas about 'race' were part of what made them special – and explore the implications of those differences. Further on, we shall try to do just that.

Most analysts, then, seem to agree that an empire is formed, most often by conquest, out of a dominant 'core' and a dominated, often economically exploited 'periphery'. These are usually geographically separate, clearly bounded places. In modern seaborne empires, they might indeed be thousands of miles apart. In other cases, though, the geographical lines between them might be blurred. Core and periphery might even be closely intermingled, inhabiting the same physical spaces: ideas like 'internal colonialism', which we shall also explore below, were developed to try to explain such situations. And it has not always been at all clear where the core ends and the periphery begins. For instance, for a considerable period Ireland was part of the United Kingdom (as a portion of it still is), and Algeria part of France. But many people in those places came to believe that they were not really treated as members – let alone equal members – of the core populations, but as parts of the colonized periphery. Many of them, moreover, decided that they did not *want* to be part of the imperial centre, even if it would have them: they wanted separation.

Such people, though, did not pursue political independence only – or, they would insist, even mainly – because they were not accepted as equals in London or Paris. They did so, they said, because they were culturally different: different enough to form a clearly separate nationality, which deserved and needed to be self-governing. As this implies, in most – maybe all – imperial systems the distinction between centre and periphery, dominant and dominated, was not just one of physical location, political power, or economic clout: it was seen in terms of cultural difference. 'Culture' is, of course, yet another of those large, baggy, rather shapeless words which this story keeps stumbling over. It is, like 'empire', 'colonialism', and our other key words, far more often invoked than defined. In modern imperial systems (and *perhaps* in many ancient ones too), however, it was typically believed that the dominant core people were clearly culturally different from, and superior to, the politically subordinate, peripheral ones. The crucial markers of difference might vary widely in different circumstances: including language, religion, physical appearance, types and levels of technology, even sexual behaviour. There was huge variation, too, as to whether imperial rulers tended to emphasize such differences or to downplay them, to see them as fixed for all time or as things that should be gradually erased by educating the colonized in the colonizers' ways. (The standard view, which is *partly* accurate, is that ancient Roman and modern French imperialists stressed the latter, the British the former.)

We shall be exploring some of these complexities, at least a little way, in later chapters. But in a place like French Algeria, the dividing lines seemed pretty clear-cut. One side was mainly Christian, French-speaking, light-skinned, comparatively prosperous; the other Muslim, Arabic or Berber-speaking, darker-skinned, and poorer. Some important groups, it is true, did not fit clearly into either camp: most obviously, Algeria's large Jewish population. But they tended to be ignored in much argument about the country's future. Indeed one of the most famous modern analyses of empire, heavily based on Algerian experience – that of Frantz Fanon – saw a total, unbridgeable chasm between the two cultures as *the* defining feature of colonial situations. Its inevitable consequence, in Fanon's view, was extreme violence.

As such conflict duly developed during the 1950s, increasingly, one side identified itself as French – even if many of these people's ancestors had actually come from places like Spain or Malta – the other as Algerian. Almost all those in the first group who had lived in Algeria chose to move, or return, to mainland France when Algeria became independent. They did so amidst much bitterness, whose legacies still haunt France, and more violently Algeria, today.

In Ireland cultural identities, and the divisions between them, seemed less sharply defined. It was far more common, and apparently easier, to think of oneself as British *and* Irish than it was to be both French and Algerian. To feel forced to choose one or the other, amidst divided affections and loyalties, was for many a painful experience. One can easily imagine a similar pain being felt by many people in Roman Britain as the legions departed. To which culture did one really belong? Where was one's true home? Indeed such a Romano-British dilemma *has* repeatedly been imagined, by literally hundreds of modern writers – especially by British ones in the later years of Britain's empire, when the drawing of parallels with the decline of Roman power became almost obsessive. A little later the theme of feeling culturally divided, even schizophrenic, torn between local tradition and colonial – then global – modernity became perhaps the most constantly recurring preoccupation of African, Asian, and other 'postcolonial' writers and artists.

Empire, it is thus suggested, always involved cultural diversity. It often rested on, and its rulers sometimes justified themselves by reference to, deep cultural divisions and inequalities. But it also inevitably produced many kinds of cultural interchange, of synthesis, mixture, or – in a word that has become exceedingly fashionable among modern students of colonialism – hybridity. For some scholars, such hybridity is its most important continuing legacy.

Others, though, question this stress on cultural legacies, as opposed to the economic or political consequences of empire. We could say indeed that there are two main lines of division and dispute among students of the modern empires: lines which overlap more than a little. One is over how much one should emphasize the power and purposefulness of colonial rulers, as against the degree of autonomy and initiative retained by the colonized. The second is about the centrality of culture to colonialism, and vice versa. Should we see modern empires as first and foremost cultural phenomena, or as political or economic ones?

Obviously enough, empire has been all these things. But some would say that another aspect was more important than any of them. Empires did not only involve rulers expanding their power, nor administrators or soldiers travelling from capital to province and money travelling in the other direction, nor even the flow of commodities, ideas, beliefs, or cultural habits from place to place. It also, nearly always, entailed the mass movement of people – even of entire peoples. Our knowledge of such movements in the ancient empires is often very sketchy, and sometimes clouded in myth. Historians nowadays tend to think that some of the 'great migrations' and even great invasions of early history may actually have involved quite small numbers of people. A few of them may never have happened at all. When the Vandals and later the Arabs swept across North Africa, or perhaps when Israelites conquered Canaan, it was not a matter of one population replacing another, but probably of a quite thin layer of new rulers superimposed on the existing inhabitants, who later, gradually, took on the culture and identity of their conquerors. At least, this happened with Arabs and Israelites: the Vandals seem to have left little by way of a cultural legacy (perhaps one of them smashed it). The cheering thing about this revised picture of ancient history is of course that, so far as it is correct, many of the mass slaughters that we read about in the Bible and elsewhere may also never have happened.

In and around the great imperial systems of modern times, the mass migrations – and sometimes the mass murders – are clearly no myth. Most obviously, they carried tens of millions of Europeans all over the globe, where they formed settler minorities (usually privileged, dominant ones) in many places, and vast majorities in others. The latter – all of North and much of South America, Australia, New Zealand, and smaller enclaves elsewhere – are sometimes, not inappropriately, called 'neo-Europes'. They form a big part of the story of modern world empire: in some ways the most important part of all. These were in the main voluntary migrations; but millions of others, especially Africans, traversed oceans and continents against their will, transported as slaves across the Atlantic – and, in a pattern far less well recorded or commemorated, the Red Sea and Indian Ocean. Somewhere in between were the vast Chinese and Indian diasporas, spreading around Asia and then the world, including traders and willing settlers but also, later, vast numbers of 'indentured labourers' whose condition was often little if any better than slavery. These were the biggest waves of migration that followed and helped form the tides of empire; but there were hundreds of other, smaller patterns. Eventually Armenian communities could be found, often as merchants, right across Eurasia, Lebanese on all the shores of the Atlantic, European Jews yet more widely spread.

Since the end of formal colonial empire, the flows of mass migration have been even more complicated and multi-directional; though they have still often followed routes first established in colonial times. And they have mostly reversed the direction of earlier imperial migrancy; going in the main from ex-colonies to former metropoles, or more broadly from poor regions to rich, from south to north, from country to city.

Still other kinds of migration are only just now beginning to receive the attention they deserve. Plants, animals, and perhaps most importantly, microbes also went everywhere that empire spread. The environmental systems of the world were transformed by what some now call ecological imperialism.

If the word 'empire' today usually carries negative overtones, then the same is even more true of 'imperialism'. It has also been even more variously defined, more fiercely and continuously argued over, than 'empire'. If an empire is a kind of object, usually a political entity, then imperialism is a process – or in some understandings, an attitude, an ideology, even a philosophy of life. That makes it inherently even harder to define than empire. Imperialism is much the newer of these words, first widely used only near the end of the 19th century. Yet entire books – rather large ones – have been written on the history of its different uses, while literally hundreds of volumes have been devoted to proposing, criticizing, or summarizing numerous rival 'theories of imperialism'.

The first uses seem, like most recent ones, to have been hostile: but unlike many of them, they were very specific. 'Imperialism' initially meant the policies of Napoleon III in France during the 1860s – his ostentatious but feeble effort to revive the glories of his mighty uncle's reign a half-century earlier. Soon, though, it started to be used to refer specifically to external policies; mainly in relation to the attitudes towards foreign affairs of British Tory Prime Minister Benjamin Disraeli and his successors. The stress on *attitudes* is important here: for most late-Victorian users of the word, imperialism did not mean the *facts* of dominance, conquest, or overseas expansion, but a policy, a philosophy, or just an emotional attitude of enthusiasm for such things. For some British critics, the label was interchangeable with 'jingoism' – a word adapted from a belligerent music-hall song and used to mean thoughtlessly aggressive patriotism. (Later an Austrian economist, Joseph Schumpeter, was to build a whole theory round the idea that imperialism stemmed from mindless aggression, expansion as an end in itself.) It was thus entirely self-consistent to say that one was opposed to imperialism, but a great friend of the British empire: many British liberal and early socialist politicians said exactly that.

Around 1890–1900, though, in Britain and elsewhere, the word started to be used by supporters as well as opponents of expansionist colonial policies. For the first and (as it soon turned out) last time, lots of people happily called *themselves* imperialists. Because of the popularity of such views – and because the period saw the rapid expansion of various European empires, especially in Africa – slightly later historians often called this the era of 'the New Imperialism' or even '*the* Age of Imperialism'. Such terminology was further encouraged by a variety of arguments, coming mainly from radical and socialist thinkers, about the relationship between colonial expansion and industrial capitalism. The most enduringly fruitful of these arguments came from the British radical-liberal

J. A. Hobson. A century later, scholarly debate on the economics of modern empire still revolves around his claim that European expansion was driven by the search for new fields of investment. Even more globally influential, though – at least so long as world Communism was a dynamic force – was Lenin's view that 'imperialism is the monopoly stage of capitalism'. Imperialism wasn't just linked to monopolistic capitalism, nor even a consequence of it – they were really one and the same thing. This had two rather pleasing implications for Communists: that by definition, only capitalist countries could be imperialists; and that, also by definition, the imperialist stage of capitalist development must be the last stage before its collapse.

Lenin's theory (or in hostile critics' eyes, his terminological conjuring trick) was widely persuasive, even for non-Marxists. This caused enduring confusion, for it was repeatedly muddled up with notions of 'imperialism' as meaning the policies of European colonial powers, or of the United States, or of any allegedly expansionist power – or just plain simple, general-purpose aggressiveness. Some writers, in slightly more discriminating fashion, use the word to mean all kinds of domination or control by one set of people over another, but especially by one state (or group of them) over others. Thus one could speak of 'formal' and 'informal' imperialism: the first meaning physical control or full-fledged colonial rule, while the second implied less direct but still powerful kinds of dominance, like Britain's 19th-century hegemony in Chile and Iran, or the USA's more recent role in much of central America.

That broad, and admittedly fuzzy-edged, definition will be used here; though we will have regularly to remind ourselves that its employment in any particular situation is always potentially contentious. What those who use the word in and about the present usually mean, however, is something like the following. A small group of powers today dominates and exploits the rest of the world. You can think of those powers in terms of states, or of economic actors (transnational companies, financial institutions, etc.) or even

– in the style of Michael Hardt and Antonio Negri – as a singular new world empire. Equally, according to ideological taste, you can characterize them as first and foremost capitalist, or as Western, white, Christian, Judaeo-Christian, secular, liberal-democratic, and so on. However described, they do form an entity, an 'it', whose undisputed leader, symbol, and greatest force is the United States. For some contemporary critics, indeed, as for orthodox Communists in the Cold War era, 'imperialism' is effectively a simple synonym for American foreign policy. It has, on this view, important continuities with the formal colonialism of the 19th and 20th centuries – indeed may share the same essential, exploitative aims – although it now operates mostly not through direct colonial rule, so much as through local client regimes, and through less formalized, less obvious economic, diplomatic, cultural, and other means of control. But when it feels its interests are threatened, it *will* intervene directly, and with massive, vindictive military force: from Vietnam in the 1960s, through Kuwait and Kosovo, to Afghanistan in 2002.

A minor oddity of modern academic – and political – language is that the word 'imperialism' has undergone a sharp decline in popularity, while 'colonialism' has zoomed up the citation charts. There are various possible reasons for this. One is that although most of the writers concerned are politically on the left, they want to distance themselves from the Marxist overtones which many understandings of 'imperialism' had accumulated – and especially from the orthodox Soviet definitions that had entered circulation via Lenin. Another might be that 'imperialism', as we've just seen, is a disagreeably muddled and fractious term, while 'colonialism' is potentially a more precise one. If that were so, it would be rather a good reason for the change. The trouble is, it *isn't* so: colonialism is being used just as variously and contentiously as imperialism ever was. Its younger relative 'postcolonialism' seems even more elastic. To some people, it's an all-purpose label for the entire state of the contemporary world. To others it's just the tag for a few Professors of English Literature, their books, and courses. Like most 'post'

words, it seems to involve coming after something – so some view
its use as dangerously misguided, for implying that colonialism is
utterly dead and done with. On the other hand, it's often unclear
just what comes after what: a recent book of literary studies is
rather mind-bendingly entitled *The Postcolonial Middle Ages*,
whilst another literary scholar suggests (admittedly with tongue
slightly in cheek) that '*Beowulf* and Chaucer's *Canterbury Tales*
could be read as postcolonial texts'.

We shall come back to the idea of the postcolonial in the final
chapter – and hopefully in a less murky fashion than that. In the
meantime, if we're to treat the current ubiquity of the label
'colonialism' as more than just an indication of how nerdishly many
academics follow fashions and repeat each other (it *is* that; but not
only that) we need to scratch a little around its roots too. 'Colony',
'colonist', 'colonial', and by extension the much more modern
'colonialism' derive, like 'empire', from Latin. Originally, a 'colony'
just meant a farming settlement; then later a place – increasingly, a
distant place – to which agricultural settlers migrated. In English
before the 19th century, a 'colony' was a place to which people
migrated, and in which they farmed: the word 'plantation' also
carried the same meaning and was used interchangeably. Thus not
all overseas possessions were called colonies: only ones where there
was substantial British settlement (which also tended, of course, to
mean places where the previous inhabitants were slaughtered or
expelled). New England and New South Wales were colonies,
Bengal or Bathurst were not.

During the late 19th and early 20th centuries, though, the meaning
shifted and widened. All distant areas subject to political rule or
control by other, mostly European, states began to be called
colonies, whether or not Europeans settled permanently there. This
remains the most common usage, and is one which this book from
now on will broadly follow. But just to uphold the general rule that
nothing in this field is straightforward, some 19th- and even 20th-
century writers carried on using the older meanings. The words

spawned an 'ism' only more recently still. Unlike imperialism and the other related words, it seems to have been used with almost exclusively hostile intent right from the start. Moreover, not only were those early uses mainly polemical, they also tended to be, deliberately, rather selective. That is, colonialism was thought of not as a system of conquest and rule, but as being a term to apply to such systems where, and only where, the conquerors were European or North American. This tendency has often been carried over into more recent, academic, and analytical uses of the word. Sometimes this is done deliberately and explicitly, by way of arguments that European or Western forms of colonialism are not just the most important kinds in modern history, but the only ones to which the term should be applied. This might be because instances of non-European countries invading, occupying, or denying rights to others are seen mostly, if not entirely, as side effects, consequences, or mere inept imitations of European and US actions. Alternatively, it might involve an argument that colonialism properly so called is a global system, whereas oppression of one Asian or African people by another has only localized consequences. Thirdly, it could be because colonialism is seen as necessarily linked to ideologies of white racial superiority or domination, which are naturally absent or very weak in 'South–South' or 'intra-Third World' conflicts.

None of these, clearly, are trivial or foolish arguments: though the first surely becomes harder to sustain the further the old European colonial empires recede into history, while the second is less plausible when the parties to 'South–South' antagonism have nuclear armouries, as with Indian–Pakistani confrontation. As for the third, there might be merit in following the suggestion of Charles W. Mills and thinking in terms of 'global white supremacy as a political system' rather than 'imperialism' or 'colonialism'. Such a description, for all its ponderousness, would capture the implied argument more accurately and less confusingly than is done by bending the concept of colonialism in yet another ideologically overburdened direction. As we shall be suggesting later, systems of colonial rule and schemata of racial thought have often been closely linked in the past few centuries – but they are not Siamese twins. They can, and often do, exist apart from one another. Indeed one lively recent book about the British empire argues that its rulers were always more concerned with social status than with race.

Most often, in any case, modern studies of empire and of colonialism do not exclude non-European conquerors on account of any of those arguments: rather, they simply forget them. For example, the frequent repression of the Kurds by the various states who have ruled them is almost never discussed using the category of colonialism. But what distinguishes the actions of the Turkish army against rebellious Kurds in the 1930s and again the 1990s, or those of Iraq in 1988, from British or French colonial-era punitive expeditions to beat up dissident tribes? The only important difference is that the Turkish and Iraqi efforts appear to have been considerably more brutal than almost any campaign on the British North-West Frontier or French West Africa; to the point of being, so many analysts have charged, genocidal in intent. To take a yet bloodier example, where again is raised the spectre of genocide, as well as the full repertoire of classic colonial justifications including the rhetoric of the 'civilizing mission', what could be a more direct descendant of 19th-century colonial conquests than Indonesia's invasion of East Timor?

The ghost of pre-modern ideas about colonies, seeing them as places of agrarian settlement, still hangs around the modern debates. Quite often, and quite confusingly, it seems to be assumed that colonial rule necessarily involves large-scale migrancy and settlement of European populations in non-European regions. In some places, of course, it did – especially the 'neo-Europes' of the Americas and south Pacific. In many others, notably most of colonial Africa and Asia, it did not. In such places, colonial domination was often exercised by a tiny handful of European soldiers and bureaucrats, plus a few traders and missionaries, none of whom intended to become permanent residents in the colony. Just as not all racism was colonial, and not all colonialism racially defined, so by no means all colonialism involved settlers – and far from all mass migration, even within the boundaries of empire, should necessarily be called colonialist. The large post-1945 movement of people from British and French colonies into the cities of the 'mother countries' is, rightly, hardly ever described in that way. And the unique, almost uniquely complex, unendingly embattled case of Palestine–Israel should remind us, if nothing else, of how complex these relationships could be.

In almost all that we have said so far, the focus has been on *states* as empire builders. Nearly always, the expanding and conquering body was indeed a state. But sometimes – especially with early-modern European overseas expansion – non-state organizations took the lead. Trading companies became conquerors and even, in effect, turned themselves into governments, maintaining armed forces, raising taxes, making and enforcing laws: the most spectacularly successful example was the British East India Company in the 18th and early 19th centuries. Yet such companies were hardly ever freelance agents: their position depended on government-granted monopolies, their functions and personnel often overlapped with or blurred into those of the state itself, and they often relied on their countries' armed forces for their ultimate defence. Most obviously, the great British colonial companies were dependent on the protection of the Royal Navy.

In the much more recent past, something rather similar has happened again, if on a smaller scale. In war-torn parts of Africa, private companies, especially those involved in mining, have become the effective rulers of substantial territories, even recruiting their own armed forces or employing mercenaries from private 'security' firms. In early 2002, the British government even floated the idea that international peacekeeping operations might be contracted out to such private bodies.

We have been following a sometimes tortuous path through a maze of arguments and definitions. We have come out, though, with what should be a set of usable, if rough-edged, concepts.

An **empire** is a large, composite, multi-ethnic or multinational political unit, usually created by conquest, and divided between a dominant centre and subordinate, sometimes far distant, peripheries.

Imperialism is used to mean the actions and attitudes which create or uphold such big political units – but also less obvious and direct kinds of control or domination by one people or country over others. It may make sense to use terms like cultural or economic imperialism to describe some of these less formal sorts of domination: but such labels will always be contentious. Some analysts also use terms like **dependency** – closely associated with economic underdevelopment – to describe these relationships. And they are clearly bound up with ideas about the newest of all these words: **globalization**. The 'anti-globalization' protestors who have confronted police forces in numerous world cities over the past few years evidently see globalization and imperialism as just two names for the same thing. Theories and rhetorics which express more positive views of the phenomenon, conversely, often tend to exaggerate the newness of the trends which they describe: the growth in transnational flows of goods, money, ideas, information, and people, with the allegedly resulting decline in the powers of the nation-state. All these have a much longer history, which scholars are only just beginning to trace. Much of this is, of course, the history of empires, which were the great transnational forces of earlier ages and the main engines of what some are now calling 'archaic' and 'early-modern' global society.

Colonialism is something more specific and strictly political: systems of rule by one group over another, where the first claims the right (a 'right' again usually established by conquest) to exercise exclusive sovereignty over the second and to shape its destiny. Usually, this political domination is 'long-distance': the rulers of one bit of land exercise rule over another, separate one, whether the latter is a neighbour or on the far side of the world. But in a few cases – perhaps including apartheid-era South Africa, and parts of Latin America – the rulers and the ruled occupied the same physical space. Terms like **internal colonialism**, though again highly contentious, may be appropriate here.

Colonization refers to large-scale population movements, where the migrants maintain strong links with their or their ancestors' former country, gaining significant privileges over other inhabitants of the territory by such links. When colonization takes place under the protection of clearly colonial political structures, it may most handily be called **settler colonialism**. This often involves the settlers entirely dispossessing earlier inhabitants, or instituting legal and other structures which systematically disadvantage them.

Finally, after the end of colonial rule, its effects still persist in innumerable different ways – though there is, of course, constant wrangling over how far various 21st-century miseries, especially in Africa, should be 'blamed' on the colonial legacy. A great range of terms has been used as collective designations for the parts of the globe once subject to colonialism: the Third World, the Less Developed (or, more optimistically, the Developing) Countries, the South, and more. The most popular today, and seemingly the most straightforward, is simply 'the **postcolonial** world'. But the straightforwardness is rather deceptive, for as we've already noted and will explore further, 'postcolonial', with its various -isms and -ities, is also employed in a bewildering variety of other ways. Another, once popular tag for what came after colonial rule is **neo-colonialism**. The term has fallen out of favour, and was always widely abused in Cold War polemics, but might still be quite useful for postcolonial situations where an outside power – usually, but not always, the former colonial ruler – still exercises very great, though half-hidden influence in ways that greatly resemble the older patterns of more open domination. France's role in some of her former African colonies comes readily to mind here.

For all these categories and concepts, there will be borderline cases, and contentious ones. For example, the indirect or informal political control exercised by the former Soviet Union over Poland, or by the United States over the Philippines, might (or might not, according to political preference) be described as imperialism. But it is not colonialism, since Poland and the Philippines retained formal political sovereignty. Nor is it colonization, since Russian or American migrants did not settle in Poland or the Philippines in significant numbers or exercise domination there. Much earlier, of course, large parts of Poland and the Philippines experienced both colonialism and colonization at the hands of Germany and Spain respectively. To take some still more controversial instances: the modern conflict in Northern Ireland is a colonial one in the eyes of Irish Republicans and of many international observers, emphatically not so in those of British governments and of Ulster Unionists. In the view of many Serbs, what happened in Kosovo in the 1990s was first a kind of creeping, but aggressive colonization by Albanians in historically Serbian land, then – when Serbs tried to defend themselves – full-scale imperialist war by the USA and its allies against Serbia. To Albanians, Kosovars, and most outside commentators, the case was entirely the reverse: the colonization, the regional imperialism, the aggression, and the guilt all lay with the Serbs, not their opponents. The Islamic militants who attacked New York and Washington on 11 September 2001 believed they were striking a blow against imperialism. To most Americans and Europeans, such a claim seemed utterly grotesque. But many people in poorer countries, even if they did not approve of these murderous acts, seemed to understand very well what the attackers said they were about. Quite obviously, defining 'empire' or 'colonialism' more precisely than these rival political forces do

PARIS EST PROPRE

GRACE A NOUS LES IMMIGRES QUI N' AIMONS PAS VOIR LES URINES ET LES CROTTES DES CHIENS
SANS NOUS, CETTE VILLE SERAIT PEUT-ETRE LA SCORIE DE CROTTES

4. *Paris is Clean* – thanks to postcolonial African and Asian migrants literally doing the dirty work. The same could have been said of almost every Western European and North American city.

won't help much in resolving their conflicts – though equally, a bit more clarity would certainly do no harm.

Therefore, even after all these attempts at clarification, the reader should beware! These are *my* stabs at definition, though naturally they draw on the ideas of many other writers. Other works, including most of those highly recommended at the end of this one, offer a huge variety of different ways of understanding the crucial concepts in the field. (And there are other books, aimed at students, with titles like 'Key Concepts in Post-Colonial Studies', which seem to me to suggest quite unhelpful and confused terminology.) Indeed no two authorities seem to agree on even the most basic issues of definition. Perhaps they never will, for the subject is so highly charged with political passions and emotion. That can make the historical study of empires frustrating, but is also part of what makes it ever-mobile and exciting.

Chapter 2
Empire by land

Empires can be categorized in all kinds of ways: ancient and modern, centralized and decentralized, ultra-brutal and relatively benign, and so on. Perhaps the most basic and important distinction, though, is between those that grew by expansion overland, extending directly outwards from original frontiers, and those which were created by sea-power, spanning the oceans and even the entire globe. The second, mainly European kind has been the most powerful and dynamic in the modern world – roughly the last 500 years. The first, land-based form of empire, however, is by far older, and has been created by more varied kinds of people: Asians, Africans, and pre-Columbian Americans as well as Europeans. It has also proved longer lasting. The European seaborne empires were almost entirely dismantled between the 1940s and the 1970s. But the Soviet state, which collapsed only in the 1990s, is seen by many as the last great land empire. Other commentators disagree, and would say that another one still exists in 2002: the vast multi-ethnic political system ruled from Beijing.

This chapter looks at the long history of land-based imperial systems, both ancient and modern. Many political systems of the ancient world are routinely described as empires – from Egypt to Babylon or the early states in what are now India and China. We shall briefly sketch the basic character of some of these, but look a little more closely at imperial Rome, since the Roman empire was a crucial influence on thinking about modern empires, and was constantly looked back to – for both inspirations and warnings – by their rulers.

Extensive political systems, far larger than the early city-states, first arose in south-west Asia about 4,000 years ago. Such states, with their powerful rulers like Sargon the Akkadian and later Hammurabi, are conventionally described as empires; and may deserve the title, in that they were created through conquest and incorporation of subject peoples, and apparently had a significant degree of centralized administration. Our strongest early evidence of deliberate, aggressive expansionism, though, comes from the Assyrians. They seem also to have developed what we might call an imperial ideology, with monuments, inscriptions, and artwork glorifying royal power, conquest, and the subjection or slaughter of 'alien' peoples. Yet historians continue to debate how far Assyrian conquests were driven by such an ideology of power, how far by economic demands, and how far by the search for defensible borders, secure against others' threats – very much the same arguments as have raged over the motivation for modern imperialism.

Between about 750 and 550 BCE, Greeks established 'colonies' around the eastern Mediterranean and the shores of the Black Sea. They were mostly small coastal settlements, apparently functioning mainly as trading posts, and though often maintaining political links with particular Peloponnesian city-states, they were self-governing: thus very unlike the colonial systems of modern times. Far larger in scale was the Persian Achaemenid empire, founded by Cyrus after 550 BCE, destroyed by Alexander in 331, but succeeded by further large-scale imperial states encompassing at different times much of what are now Iran, Iraq, Turkey, Syria, and beyond. It is sometimes argued that this polity's conflicts with Greeks, and their depiction by Greek writers, were the crucial point of origin for 'Orientalist' stereotypes and prejudices, contrasting, for instance, Greek (and by extension Western or European) freedom with Asian despotism, Greek hardihood with Asiatic degeneracy.

Where huge, multi-ethnic empires were created in the ancient world, they were often extremely unstable and short-lived: Egypt, where the confining geography of the Nile valley almost enforced a kind of unifying stability, was the greatest exception. Vast imperial systems could be created, and then collapse, within a single short lifetime: that built by Alexander in the 320s BCE lasted less than a decade. Such empires were, it seems, most often built by invaders or settlers from outside the areas concerned: or at least, subsequent legend depicted it that way. The reality is often far less clear, and in many cases has been the subject of centuries of controversy. Thus we have a fairly well-known early narrative of ancient state-building between the Mediterranean and the River Jordan: the biblical story of Hebrew migration and conquest. But almost nothing in the archaeological record supports that story. We have had centuries of argument over the sources of Greek civilization: was it purely local, the creation of invaders from the north, or of colonists from Africa and Asia, or of far more complex, multi-directional flows of cultural influence? For many modern polemicists, this comes down to a fruitless but emotionally charged wrangle over whether the original Greeks were 'white' or not. Somewhat similarly, argument over who created the first great states in the Indian subcontinent, and the idea of India itself, is embroiled in modern nationalist assertions, religious rivalries, and 'racial' claims: was it indigenous peoples, 'Aryan' invaders from the north, or much later Muslim or even British conquerors? At the time of writing, India's ultra-nationalist present government is trying to impose its own idiosyncratic version of ancient history on school textbooks. It seems especially obsessed with removing from them the scandalous suggestion that ancient Indians might not have held cows holy, and may even have eaten beef.

Not only were many of these ancient empires fragile and often transient, but they were also, in the main, far more limited in their powers than their rulers' boasts implied. Those powers were mostly confined to waging war and levying taxes – or indeed

5. The clash of ancient empires: Alexander and Darius at the battle of Issus. Mosaic from Pompeii.

exacting tribute by more or less crude, forcible, and inefficient means. Very few seem to have succeeded, or even tried, in imposing a uniform system of law and order, let alone a common culture, on their scattered subjects. Almost everything centred on the person, the household, the family, and retainers of the ruler himself. There was rarely any clear distinction between his personal strength, fortunes, and finances and those of the state: which is of course partly why so many could not survive the death of a great individual founder or conqueror. The limited nature of imperial rule must also have meant that the dramatic, even seemingly cataclysmic political events of imperial conquest or collapse, invasion or dynastic change actually made rather little difference to the lives of the majority of people. The Roman, Chinese, and perhaps ancient Egyptian states were partial exceptions to this generalization: they, far more than most, seem to have established bureaucracies, legal systems, and a degree of cultural diffusion which made their impact on everyday life deeper and more enduring than most other empires could achieve. In the Roman case especially, this enabled the empire's cultural influence to endure – not least through religious institutions – far beyond its own political demise.

In Africa, at least outside the Nile valley, large-scale, multi-ethnic state creation was rarer, and when it happened even more fragile. Most of the continent remained relatively thinly populated and farmable land abundant, so state power could be evaded if it grew too onerous, simply by migration. Control over territory mattered less than control of labour and of long-distance trade. Major monarchical states including large urban centres were created, especially in west-central Africa – certainly far more so than later European stereotypes suggested – but they were untypical of the continent's political forms; and even where such existed, the term 'empire' is only loosely applicable. Later, more extensive state formation – again especially in West Africa – was strongly driven by outside influences: the spread of Islam, availability of firearms and war-horses, and most destructively by competition to control the supply of slaves for the Atlantic trade. Elsewhere and later still, fiercely ambitious warrior kings – the most famous instance was the Zulu founder-monarch Shaka – rapidly built new, extensive states by conquest. Terms like 'empire-building' are sometimes used by historians for these processes; but again, the label is only loosely applicable.

In north-eastern Africa, the story was rather different: though the difference may sometimes be exaggerated by an entrenched but dubious habit of viewing Egypt's history in total isolation from the rest of Africa. Even more dubious was a tendency – now largely discredited – to see the Pharaonic state's southward expansion as especially similar to modern imperialism because, supposedly, it involved conquest by 'white' Egyptians of 'black' Nubians. This is quite misleading. There is no evidence that these ancient peoples had anything like modern 'racial' concepts; and the relationships between Egypt and Nubia were not all one way in terms of trade or even of conquest. Yet the ancient Egyptian monarchy was undoubtedly the most powerful and far the longest-lasting state of the time, and although it rarely displayed the kind of expansionist drive found in Assyria or later in Rome, it did at times rule extensive territories outside its own heartland. With Egypt's decline, large-scale monarchical states grew or persisted in what is now Sudan (Napata and Meroe) and in Ethiopia. In the latter, the resulting Abyssinian 'empire' could be seen, with the more spectacularly successful Chinese case, as a major instance of archaic imperialism persisting and renewing itself into modern times, even despite European incursions.

Similarly across most of the Americas, large-scale, multi-ethnic, centralized state systems seem to have been rare before European conquest. The major exceptions were in the central isthmus and the Andes, where during the first millennium CE the Maya, Huari, and Tiahanaco civilizations extended over wide areas – though they may have had little political unity, so again the term 'empires' can only be used very loosely. It might be more appropriate for the apparently more unified states created in the second millennium CE: the Toltec, then the Aztec in Mexico, the Inca in Peru. Yet none of these formed a unitary or stable political entity. When the Spaniards came, they destroyed the American empires with astonishing ease: partly by superior weaponry, partly through their own extreme ruthlessness, but partly because they could exploit the bitter divisions among local peoples and the resentments of those who had been conquered by Aztecs or Inca.

Outside western Asia and the Mediterranean world, by far the most striking instance of ancient empire-building was in what is now China. Some trace the growth of extensive states in northern China as far back as the Shang and successor Chou 'kingdoms', well over 3,000 years ago; but it is doubtful if these were really more than loose federations of much smaller polities, with little real central authority. Here, as with the even older Harappan civilization in India, the idea of a vast ancient empire owes more to modern nationalism than to the archaeological record. Only under the Qin (or Ch'in) and then Han dynasties, in the two centuries immediately before the Christian era, was China largely unified. And although most of the south Asian peninsula was briefly united first by Hindu and Buddhist conquerors in the 3rd century BCE, then by Muslim ones in the 13th century, none of these 'empires' encompassed the entire region, and none proved able to sustain themselves for more than a few generations.

China aside, the ancient empire which was, by far, to have the greatest continuing world influence was the Roman. The central Italian city-state's expansion began about 500 BCE. Two centuries later, it controlled almost all Italy; 300 years after that, the entire Mediterranean world, south-west Asia and much of Western Europe. It could be said that the Romans invented the concept of empire, at least in the forms in which it was to be understood, and constantly referred back to, by later empire builders.

The system rested on exploitation: tribute in cash, in kind, or in slaves sent from the peripheries to the imperial centre. Some contemporaries, and many later historians, believed that this reliance on subject peoples to pay for the empire, to sustain the relative wealth (and thus the supposed idleness and decadence) of the rulers, and increasingly to fight their wars for them too, gradually undermined Roman power and led to the empire's collapse. Power waned because the will to power atrophied. Loss of frugal republican virtue led to loss of strength. Such ideas were to be revived time and again in the succeeding centuries; perhaps most influentially in Renaisssance Italy, but also in 20th-century Britain as its empire declined.

Yet Romans clearly also believed in what a later imperial age would call their 'civilizing mission'. Indeed that very language owes a great deal to Roman writers like Cicero, who asserted that *only* under Roman rule could civilization flourish. Their language, learning, and literature – and, 'piggybacking' on Roman power, those of the Greeks – were spread across the entire Mediterranean world and beyond. From Wales to Syria people, at least among the upper classes, came to build very similar houses, wear similar clothes, eat much the same food, and watch the same rather cruel games. The rights of citizenship, and even the opportunity to rule, were gradually extended to people who were not of Roman or Italian birth. I have suggested that for a political system aptly to be called an empire at all, it must in some way have been 'multi-ethnic' or 'multinational'. But to apply such criteria to the ancient world is, of course, to use language which is both very modern and highly contested. Some historians think that we should not refer to 'nationalism' in relation to any period before the past 200 years or so. But we can surely, without gross anachronism, speak of Rome's empire as a multi-ethnic or multicultural one, but also one where what a later age would call cultural assimilationism was vigorously practised and widely accepted.

Romans even, uniquely among ancient empire builders, left record of what appear to be anti-imperialist protest by those they conquered. All, however, come to us through Roman authors – and may have been dreamed up entirely by them: a letter purportedly from Mithridates King of Pontus, composed by Sallust, and two speeches supposedly made by legionary mutineer Percennius and British chief Calgacus, recorded (or composed) by Tacitus. A phrase from Calgacus' supposed oration has had lasting resonance: the Romans, he says, 'create a wasteland, and call it peace'. Some Romans, it seems from this, sympathized with the victims of their conquests, and had the imagination to see how cruel and oppressive it might appear to them. They could apparently even encompass the view that rule by one people over another is wrong in principle. Yet some observers suspect that Tacitus and Sallust actually had quite different intentions, and wanted their readers to respond by thinking: 'See how foolish these barbarians are, ranting and railing against the might – and the obvious advantages – of our rule.' And for all that we know, Calgacus' supposed words are a purely imaginary concoction, just like the image of another semi-mythical British 'freedom fighter' against Rome, Boadicea, which stands outside Britain's Parliament.

Beyond these often fragile or fissiparous political units something far larger, and in many ways more important, grew up in antiquity: a pattern of trade and cultural interaction extending from the shores of the Atlantic to those of the Pacific and the Yellow Sea. We have clear evidence of trading and cultural contact right across the Eurasian continent (the idea that it's really *two* continents, Europe and Asia, is a far more recent invention) over 2,000 years ago; and some rather speculative historians would push the story much further back than that. In some eyes at least, it amounted to a single civilizational complex or 'world system'. If so, it does not seem to have extended significantly into sub-Saharan Africa until much later – though there are still huge gaps in our knowledge here. Nor (leaving aside a handful of Viking voyagers, and a mass of legends) did it yet include the Americas, or the islands of the south Pacific. Australia's inhabitants probably remained more isolated from

43

6. Resisters: Queen Boadicea: statue outside Palace of Westminster, London.

outside influence than any other major human group, until the cataclysmic European impact in the 18th century.

It should also be borne in mind that although political empires were built mostly by expansion overland, economic and cultural influences spread at least as much by sea. The various shores of the Mediterranean, of the Indian Ocean, and (perhaps more tentatively) of the eastern Atlantic were in many ways far more closely bound together than were Eurasia's land masses. Finally, if there was a 'chain' of empires stretching across the Eurasian world of 2,000 or of 1,500 years ago, we should not necessarily see the westernmost of these, the Roman empire, as the most important. In the long run, ideas from and about Rome were indeed to shape the modern world more decisively than any others. But in 700 or even in 1700 CE, the successive Chinese empires were more politically unified, more populous, more prosperous, and by most measures more technologically advanced than anything further west. They also had wider-ranging networks of trade and influence. China probably contained about one third of the world's total population, and controlled or participated in an even higher proportion of its long-distance trade. There has been a great deal of argument about 'Eurocentrism' in modern history: but for centuries, if anywhere could stake a real claim to be the centre of the world, it was China. Indeed China's rulers thought of themselves as being just that: theirs was 'the Middle Kingdom' – and still in 1756, Voltaire began his *Essaie sur l'histoire générale* with China. The age of European dominance, and of European world empire, was still to come – but first it would be south-west Asia's turn, under the inspiration of an astonishingly dynamic new state-building religious creed.

By the early 9th century CE, the Islamic Abbasid Caliphate – heir to the startlingly rapid expansion of Islam in the years following the Prophet's death – was by far the largest state in the world, extending from Africa's Atlantic coast to the Pamir mountains and Indus river. Its nearest rival for size was T'ang China. Further west and north, the European, mainly Christian empires of the Byzantines, the Carolingians, and the short-lived Bulgarian and Khazar polities seemed petty, almost 'provincial' entities by comparison. Yet Abbasid power too proved ephemeral. The Islamic world could not be sustained as a single political unit, though this was a frequently revived dream or aspiration. Culturally, however, a considerable degree of unity was sustained: not only through the shared (if, of course, also internally disputatious) faith itself, but through widespread literacy in Arabic and a wide range of cultural practices from types of cooking to ways of celebrating marriage. These practices, indeed, came to be widely embraced also by non-Muslim minorities in Islamic-ruled areas.

Nor was the political dynamism of the Abbasid empire's smaller successor states by any means exhausted. The most powerful of them, the Ottoman empire centred on modern Turkey, dominated the eastern Mediterranean, gradually undermined the ailing Byzantine empire, and battered at the gates both of Vienna and of Malta, keys to central and to south-west Europe respectively. This was certainly not a matter of a single, clear-cut, centuries-long conflict between 'East' and 'West' or between Christians and Muslims. There were alliances between the camps and of course bitter struggles within each of them, while the flows of trade and of cultural influence across the supposed great divide never ceased. Yet even so, the idea of an epochal 'clash of civilizations', however mythicized, profoundly shaped many people's thinking then and since – and it has had a dramatic revival in the early 21st century.

Here, once again, we encounter politically charged problems over use of terms like imperialism and colonialism. Some historians would describe the series of European invasions of south-west Asia usually labelled the Crusades – which were partly, but *only* partly, motivated by religious fervour – as an early, perhaps the earliest, expression of Western colonial aggression against non-Europeans. Indeed in a much later era of conflict between some Islamic states and Western alliances, radical Islamists took to describing Israelis, or American forces in the Gulf, as latter-day Crusaders; while the greatest Arab foe of the Crusades, Salah ad-Din (who was actually a Kurd) was invoked by Iraqis, Palestinians, and others as a latter-day hero and symbol. Some other modern commentators (though fewer of them) would call the converse process, the attempts by the Ottoman empire to conquer Europe, an Islamic imperialism. Modern hatred against Muslim communities in south-eastern Europe, notably in Bosnia and Kosovo, has often been articulated in terms of seeing them as unwelcome residues of this imperialism: in short, as 'Turks'.

Almost as dramatic as the expansion of Islamic-ruled, multinational empire after the 7th century was the Mongol explosion in the 13th and 14th. Under Genghis Khan (c.1167–1227) and his successors, their rule briefly stretched from central Europe to China. But it, too, rapidly proved impossibly overextended and fragile. The briefly all-conquering and culturally rich state forged by Timur in central and south-west Asia in the late 14th century was its last great flowering. It had, though, a major posthumous offshoot further south and east: for descendants of Timur – Babur and Akbar – created the Mughal state which ruled most of India from the early 16th century. This was the nearest thing to a unified India ever created, except under the British Raj: though still not, perhaps, a *very* near thing. And although later Hindu nationalists were to decry these Muslim overlords as brutal oppressors, the record suggests rather the reverse. Akbar's reign was religiously tolerant, culturally effervescent, and humane – at least by the rather lax standards one must apply to emperors. His successors, though, were less impressive; and the Mughal system was disintegrating even before it was seriously challenged by new contenders for power in south Asia: the Portuguese, French, and then British.

Further west, nothing comparable to the vast Chinese, Abbasid, Mongol, or Byzantine states emerged for many centuries after the fall of Rome. Europe developed much smaller, more numerous

7. **Imperialists:** The Emperor Timur receiving his grandson Pir Muhammad. The former 'barbarian' conqueror now rules peacefully amidst all the trappings of Islamic imperial high culture – and has time for the family.

political units: but though this might be a source of short-term, especially military weakness, it is often suggested that in relative fragmentation lay the sources of future advantage. Even so, more limited processes of empire-building dominated the medieval history of Western Europe too: so much so that this entire story can be seen as one of conquest and colonization. The rulers and ideas of 'Latin Europe' – Catholic, Franco-German, based on the new military technologies of heavy cavalry and castle-building – expanded dramatically from the 11th century onwards. The same aggressive, self-confident aristocratic class, mostly originating in northern France, which conquered England, took over Scotland and attempted the conquest of Wales and Ireland, was at the same time seizing control of Sicily and Spain, Bohemia and Silesia, even Cyprus and Palestine. The Celtic and Anglo-Saxon peoples of the west were in this sense colonized subjects, just as many Slavic groups were in the east and Mediterranean peoples to the south. By 1350, there were 15 Catholic monarchs in Europe. Some were related to one another, so ten families held the crowns of Europe. No fewer than seven of the ten, controlling 12 kingdoms, were of Frankish origin. They included the kings of England, Scotland, Spain, Portugal, Bohemia, southern Italy, Sicily, and Cyprus. Only Denmark, Sweden, and Poland had 'local' ruling families. One aspect of this expansion which was to have especially bloody long-term consequences was German eastward colonization from about 1125 onwards. Military colonization by the Teutonic Knights in Poland and the Baltic states – dignified with the title of a 'Crusade', like its equivalents further south and east – was followed by large-scale settlement of traders and farmers. Only in the mid-20th century was this to be reversed, amid enormous trauma.

Thus despite the political fragmentation, much of Europe possessed important elements of a common culture, at least among members of the ruling groups – it was, one could say, that commonality which produced the very idea of Europe. The Church and the use of Latin were naturally crucial in this, and became ever more so. But in secular ruling circles too a kind of network of understanding and shared values increasingly existed: the three great rivals for the English crown in 1066, Harold Godwinson, Harald Hardrada, and William the Bastard, obviously understood one another very well. Apart from anything else, they all shared Scandinavian ancestry. This 'Aristocrats' International', which in changed forms remained a factor in European politics and culture at least until the era of the French Revolution, in some ways evidently worked *against* the development of national identities. It emphasized 'lateral' links between members of the same class rather than 'vertical' cross-class national solidarities. It meant that there were no insuperable barriers to ruling groups from one place acclimatizing to and mingling with those of suitable social standing from another. This made early state-building within Europe very different from attempts at expansion beyond.

Modern land empires

Some of the great land-based empires soon became little more than vague memories. Five of them, though, lasted into the 20th century: the Ottoman, Russian, Austro-Hungarian, Chinese, and American.

The Ottoman empire was in many ways an anomaly, at least in the later centuries of its long existence. To many Europeans its very presence in the modern era was peculiar – a gigantic Asian, Muslim-ruled polity in a world otherwise dominated by Europe, existing in a state of long-term, irreversible decay. To many, it only managed to survive at all by allying with some European powers against others: first France and Britain against Russia, then Germany against the Western allies. Its Anatolian 'heartland', far from growing fat on tribute from the periphery, was poorer and more economically backward than almost any other part. All the other modern empires – including those of liberal, commercial Britain and even republican France – were to a great extent run by and for aristocracies. The Ottoman system had no hereditary aristocracy, and its rulers worked hard to make sure that one did not arise. Indeed for most of its history much of the bureaucracy and

8. **Imperialists: Mehmed the Conqueror, Ottoman emperor 1451–81.**
The Ottoman empire was at its most dynamically expansionist under his
rule. Yet the fact of his sitting for a European-style portrait painting
hints at the cultural interchange which persisted through the wars of his
era.

army, including senior officials, was composed of people who, in terms of formal status at least, were slaves. 'Non-aristocratic', however, certainly did not mean 'modern and efficient'. By comparison with the major European states or even with Russia, the Ottomans increasingly failed at the two most basic tasks of government, raising revenue and maintaining a monopoly of effective armed force. The empire's rule in the peripheries was often corrupt, seemingly inept, sometimes brutally repressive. Yet it was certainly more tolerant, especially of religious difference, than its European counterparts. That relative tolerance doubtless helped the system to survive for as long as it did. So, perhaps paradoxically, did the very weakness of central control, which allowed considerable freedom of action to local notables.

Although outsiders often called the empire 'Turkish', its ruling elites were ethnically diverse, and thought of themselves in religious far more than in national terms. This too, in a world increasingly defined and divided by nation-state identities, made the Ottomans seem like anachronisms. Some historians argue indeed that it was when the empire's new rulers tried to modernize, near the end of the 19th century and then more forcefully under the 'Young Turks' after 1908, that they opened the way to the destruction of their own power – not least because that modernization included attempts to create a 'Western-style' Turkish nationalism, which almost inevitably produced reactive nationalist upsurges among the subject peoples. Many of these received backing from various European states. The empire's response mixed conciliation and repression – including, in its last days, a genocidal onslaught against the Armenian minority – but was increasingly ineffective. Defeat in the 1914–18 war brought the whole system crashing down, but perhaps only hastened a collapse which was in process anyway.

If Ottoman decline appeared to many observers to be inevitable throughout the 19th century, some saw Russia's rise to pre-eminence as equally fated. The first Russian state was founded –

mainly by Scandinavian settlers – in the late 9th century; but more than once collapsed into smaller, rival units. Only after the 1480s did a partly reunified Russia, centred now on Moscow rather than Kiev, begin the slow process of growth east and south. For centuries, it was seen as economically weak and socially 'backward' in comparison both to the European states to its west and China to its south-east. Much of its history was dominated by fierce debates over how to catch up, between 'Slavophiles' who asserted Russia's totally unique character and destiny, and 'Westernizers' who tried to turn it into another England, France, or Prussia. Yet pre-revolutionary Russia was also, of course, itself an expansionary imperial power. By the start of the 20th century, its land area was probably the greatest of any imperial system, not only at the time but ever – though a great deal of it was almost uninhabited. If the empire's western heartland stood in a relation of stigmatized inferiority to North Atlantic capitalism, then its Asian colonies were yet further behind in the imagined hierarchy. Russian intellectuals lamented their country's inferiority to 'the West', but simultaneously saw themselves as carriers of modern civilization to Siberia, central Asia, and the Caucasus. The mixture was remarkably closely echoed by later Soviet ideologues as they undertook their own 'civilizing mission' yet further afield.

For those 'Westernizers', whether liberals or Marxists, who measured Tsarist Russia against European models, it was bound to be found wanting. Its governing machinery was top-heavy, cumbersome, grossly inefficient, its political system autocratic, its agriculture primitive, its industry underdeveloped. Yet the empire possessed not only vast natural and human resources, but considerable dynamism. Some historians argue, with much evidence in support, that before 1914 Russia was poised for 'take-off' into rapid economic development. The 1917 revolution, on this view, did not make Russia a modern industrial power: it merely delayed that process, and then shackled it with Communist central planning.

And as it expanded, the Russian empire proved able to employ a range of methods of rule, with the flexibility which all successful empires had to learn. At the centre, almost all power was indeed concentrated on the Tsar and the top aristocracy. Russian conquests in Asia were certainly no less brutal than those of any other expanding imperial power. But on the peripheries, collaborative alliances – even systems of 'Indirect Rule' – were forged with non-Russian elites: not only local nobles but also Islamic religious leaders in central Asia, or Baltic and German-speaking bourgeois. The great mistake of the Tsars' last ministers, perhaps, was that they tried too precipitately to move away from this policy at the start of the 20th century. This was partly in pursuit of rationalizing, modernizing reform, partly because – very much in line with trends elsewhere – the state was increasingly associating itself with an idea of ethnic Russianness. As with Spain in the Americas a century earlier and the Young Turks around the same time, attempts to centralize and reform imperial rule instead contributed to its collapse. Lenin and the Bolsheviks were able to appeal successfully to the resulting discontents on the periphery, and won the Civil War in large part for that reason – even though their promises of greater freedom for peripheries and minorities proved false. Somewhat similar tensions were to undermine Gorbachev's attempts at far-reaching reform 70 years later. And they have not vanished under his post-Communist successors. The Russian empire finally disintegrated in the 1990s, as Soviet ideology did. Its ending was largely bloodless, at least in the first instance: but territorial rivalries and civil conflicts festered in several of the successor states. Russia itself remained embroiled in a bitter war – in many eyes a clearly colonialist one – in Chechnya. Many ethnic Russians, struggling amidst bleak economic conditions and bewildered by the loss of great-power status, harboured an obvious nostalgia for empire. Extreme nationalist politicians sought to play on such feelings; and in the early 21st century, few would be bold enough to predict that the age-old Russian expansionist drive would never be renewed.

The Habsburg empire, like the Russian, began to be forged in the 16th century, and expanded as Ottoman power waned in the 17th and 18th. Shaken by attempted revolution in 1848, and thereafter by military defeat, the breakaway of its Italian possessions and the rise of Prussia, it responded – unlike almost any other of the older empires – with far-reaching, largely successful reform. The Hungarian half of its 'Dual Monarchy' was given wide-ranging autonomy, the Czech lands (which were the empire's most economically vigorous region) and the other Slavic territories lesser but steadily growing civic rights.

The Austro-Hungarian empire has had a bad press. Nationalist leaders among its minority peoples scorned it as the 'prison-house of nations'. To members of the extraordinarily creative intellectual and artistic circles in Vienna, it was pretty self-evident that the state under which they lived was a senile absurdity. Yet the very existence of those nationalist, cultural, and intellectual movements, able to express their damning criticisms with largely unrestricted freedom, hints at a more positive story. Of course the empire never solved its immensely complex nationalities problem, made more difficult by the fact that so many of its subjects – Italians, Poles, Serbs, even the politically dominant German-speakers – were linked to states outside its borders, with which some yearned for unity. However, its efforts at achieving peaceful coexistence through a pluralist, 'multicultural' policy (for instance sponsoring education in all the empire's languages) were strenuous, and in many ways ahead of their time.

None other of the great modern empires shared power more widely among its constituent peoples, and none came closer to achieving something which was perhaps an impossibility, a contradiction in terms: sustaining a multinational empire which was also a democracy. The Habsburg system was not fully democratic: no European, or other, country was before 1918. Britain, France, the USA, and even Germany before 1914 had somewhat more broadly representative and liberal polities than did Austro-Hungary. But none of them extended those quasi-democratic rights to their subject peoples, to the imperial peripheries. The Habsburg Dual Monarchy did so, at least to a substantial degree. Even the Irish nationalist leader Arthur Griffith saw the Dual Monarchy as an idea to be emulated in British–Irish relations. Modern historians who urge that it should be revalued as a noble, precocious effort at multicultural and multinational harmonization, strikingly akin to the European Union today, are idealizing more than a little. But in comparison with most of its rival imperial systems, and certainly compared to the dictatorship, war, ethnic cleansing, and even genocide which many of its subject peoples suffered after it had gone, it deserves some retrospective applause, even a small sigh of regret for its passing.

China is rarely considered among the great modern empires. Yet as we have seen, for centuries it had been not only a vast, multi-ethnic polity – clearly fitting most historians' definitions of an imperial system – but the world's most populous, prosperous, and by many measures most sophisticated society. Its story in the 19th and earlier 20th centuries was largely one of decline. Although it escaped full-scale European colonial occupation – and, after 1937, successfully resisted Japanese attempts at conquest – the degree of weakness, dependence, and foreign penetration was such that by the end of the Victorian era, it was commonplace to describe China's status as 'semi-colonial'. But many Chinese, especially among the ruling elites, remained just as convinced that theirs was the only true civilization, all others barbarians, as were the Romans, or the 19th-century West Europeans. The continued strength of Chinese national sentiment was evident in successive movements of revolt and reform, from the 'Boxer' rebellion in 1900, through Sun Yat-Sen's republicanism, to the rise of a distinctively, indeed aggressively, Chinese version of Communism. It was expressed, perhaps, even more powerfully in the immense strength of a centralizing, culturally homogenizing state bureaucracy which, although it came near to breakdown amidst invasion and civil war in the first half of the 20th century, was revived, at least as strong as ever, under Mao Zedong. Some analysts suggest that the Chinese idea of empire was never expansionist in the way that either European or Islamic ones were, perhaps because its core values were those of that civilian bureaucracy, not of the military or aristocracy. Others, though, argue that the alleged Chinese aggression against Vietnam and the continuing, classically colonialist drive to eradicate Tibetan culture point to a very different evaluation.

To describe the United States as a 'great land-based empire' is also controversial, and may seem to some even perverse. Some early American writers and politicians did indeed refer to their newly sovereign country as an 'empire' – but that was because, classically educated and self-consciously backward-looking as so many of them were, they had in mind early Roman ideas of 'empire' as meaning simply 'state'. Their models too, like slightly earlier Spanish or British rulers', were Roman, from Senate and Capitol downwards. And when, from the late 19th century, radical and dissident American writers began to attack their country's policies for drifting towards empire, they meant mainly its overseas expansionism in places like Cuba and the Philippines and – classically-minded again – tendencies to internal autocracy and corruption. A little later still, and up to the present, the dominant notion of American empire is one of trade, finance, and cultural influence, largely without formal colonies or permanent conquests. Yet it is the internal expansion of the continental USA, across the intervening hundred years, which evokes the most direct parallels with empire-building elsewhere. Exterminatory war, 'freelance' expansionism by adventurers, farmers, prospectors, and religious fanatics, ecological devastation, the drawing up of oft-broken treaties and protectorates, experiments in Indirect Rule and drives for cultural assimilation – all featured at one time or another, just as they did in British, French, or Russian imperialisms. If the modern USA had few of the distinctively imperial problems within its own borders which haunted the other great land empires, that was largely because the earlier conquest had been almost uniquely

9. Resisters: Tatanka-Iyotanka – Sitting Bull – is one of the few fighters against colonial rule to be remembered as an individual, and also one of the few to have had some success in battle against the invaders.

complete. More totally than anywhere else since the first Spanish invasions of the Americas, native peoples were physically destroyed or marginalized. Despite a few legal victories over land rights at the end of the 20th century, that marginalization remains largely in force.

Some historians and political analysts assert that the US polity manifested 'colonial' features beyond its treatment of indigenes. Certainly in the aftermath of the 1860s Civil War, the Reconstruction-era northern policy towards the south had many of the classic features of a colonial occupation – albeit one whose short-term impact was clearly beneficial to the former slaves and indeed to poor whites. Later, it was occasionally argued that the situation of African-Americans, as an exploited minority with, at least in some eyes, the characteristics of a distinct nation, was one of 'internal colonialism' within the USA. Various groups, including US Communists and militant black nationalists, argued from this that African-Americans should seek a sovereign country of their own or even a revolution. Yet these were mostly small groups: the notion of Afro-America as an internal colony never seemed either as analytically powerful nor as popular as equivalent ideas did in South Africa or parts of Latin America.

During the 20th century all the major land-based empires dwindled or collapsed – though China's then underwent partial revival, while the USA's West arguably only ceased to be imperial precisely because the drive for empire was so complete a success. The mid-century, however, also witnessed the shortest-lived, most dramatic, and most destructive modern attempt to create a land-based territorial empire: Germany's drive for eastward *lebensraum*. Hitler repeatedly said that Russia would be for his Germany what India was for Britain: which suggests that he knew very little about India. The post-war order which Hitler and, more single-mindedly, Heinrich Himmler planned for Eastern Europe was to involve vast movements of population and planned resettlement, quite unlike British India. Millions of Germans were to become colonists in the east, ruling over indigenous populations reduced to slave-labour status. Those unworthy even of that status – most obviously, the Jews – and those who might potentially challenge the new order, like Polish and Russian intellectuals, would be eliminated altogether. Elsewhere, though, in the Baltic and the Balkans, an Indirect Rule system of client regimes would be established. The eastern colonies would not only be a vast field for settlement, but a reservoir of raw materials, agricultural products, and cheap labour for Germany.

The whole idea was an explicitly colonial one, drawing on ideas about ancient Rome as well as on the most brutal aspects of modern European empire-building: indeed many veterans of Germany's pre-1918 African colonial administrations were drafted into Himmler's SS. The actual implementation, in the short time that this monstrous experiment could run, was unsurprisingly chaotic as well as ferocious. It was also in many ways counter-productive. Hitler had not learnt one of the most basic lessons of earlier, successful, imperialisms: the need to co-opt rather than alienate, let alone massacre, conquered elites. Yet many historians concur that the economic exploitation of the Nazi-conquered lands was surprisingly, indeed disconcertingly, efficient – as of course was the industralized slaughter of Jews. One consequence of Hitler's failure was to undo another, much older pattern of intra-European colonization. As we have seen, German-speaking settlers had spread across central eastern Europe since the early Middle Ages. With the Nazi collapse, most of their descendants fled or were expelled. The only consolation for their sufferings – which, though not as terrible as those the Nazis had inflicted, were still immense – was that most of them, as citizens of the new Germany, undoubtedly ended up richer than if they had stayed put.

The Nazis' project, then, was a clearly colonialist one: only more sweepingly savage, so most observers agreed, than any other before it. Yet some, like the French Caribbean poet and politician Aimé Césaire, questioned that last judgement. They argued forcefully that

Nazi racial policy and even genocide had many colonial precursors. They aroused such condemnation only because, for the first time, such things were being done to white people within Europe rather than in distant colonies. We shall look later at accusations of colonial genocide, and the question of whether European actions in some colonies were parallels or precedents for the Nazi Holocaust.

It should be possible for us to control this region to the East with two hundred and fifty thousand men plus a cadre of good administrators. Let's learn from the English, who with two hundred and fifty thousand men in all, including fifty thousand soldiers, govern four hundred million Indians. This space in Russia must always be dominated by Germans.

Nothing would be a worse mistake on our part than to seek to educate the masses there. It is to our interest that the people should know just enough to recognise the signs on the roads. At present they cannot read, and they ought to stay like that . . .

We'll supply the Ukrainians with scarves, glass beads and everything that colonial peoples like. The Germans – this is essential – will have to constitute amongst themselves a closed society, like a fortress. The least of our stable-lads must be superior to any native. For German youth, this will be a magnificent field of experiment.

Adolf Hitler, *Table Talk* 27 July and 17 September 1942. (ed. Hugh Trevor-Roper, Oxford, 1988; orig. pub. 1953), pp. 15, 34

In fact Hitler grossly overestimated the number of British officials who ran India. Apart from the army, there were only about 12,000 of them in the 1930s.

Chapter 3
Empire by sea

Here the rise of the 'long-distance' overseas imperialisms of the
Western European powers will be sketched. These – and especially
the British empire – have come to be seen as the classic forms of
imperialism: and indeed most books on the subject confine
themselves to the European seaborne empires. What, though, was
distinctive about them? Earlier histories usually stressed how
colonial expansion was driven by money and power – including
power struggles within and between European states. More
recently, attention has shifted to empire as a cultural phenomenon.

Medieval Europe, we have suggested, was politically fragmented,
economically backward, and culturally unsophisticated by
comparison with the great Islamic, Chinese, and other empires to
its east. Yet from the late 15th century onwards, it rose from
provinciality to global dominance. At the peak of its strength
European colonial powers, plus their offshoot the United States,
ruled well over 80 per cent of the world's land, and effectively
controlled all the oceans too.

This unprecedented burst of growth was, of course, an enormously
complex process. Very briefly and crudely, the dominant seagoing
imperial powers in the first phase of expansion – roughly between
the first voyages to America and the European Thirty Years War –
were Spain and Portugal. Their major colonizing efforts were in the

Americas, where Spain rapidly became the dominant power; but the Portuguese also established a presence – still more as traders than as conquerors – at scattered points on the African and south Asian coasts. Increasingly in the later 16th and early 17th centuries, they were challenged by others: by France, which was recovering from a long period of weakness and from its own religious civil wars, and bidding to become Europe's dominant power; by the Dutch, who had just successfully broken away from Spanish overrule; and by England, which was certainly not a major player in intra-European conflicts, but was increasingly powerful at sea. These countries too directed their main early efforts towards the Americas – though much of England's expansionist energy was exerted much closer to home, in the effort to dominate Ireland and Scotland. Both Spanish and Portuguese power went into long-term decline, with their military and naval resources overextended and their domestic economies stagnating.

This expansion always depended, in the last resort, on the power of the European states – which became far more efficient tax-gathering and war-waging machines than anything else the world had yet seen. Yet a great deal of it was carried out, especially among the English and the Dutch, by private enterprise. Powerful merchant companies drove the process forward, and on the outermost fringe or cutting edge of empire, the aggressive initiative often came from a bizarre mixture of adventurers, freebooters, and pirates. The later popular images of piracy often see it as enshrining an anarchic kind of freedom, with pirate crews and settlements as havens of resistance to the authority of the imperial state. Some modern historians share this rather romantic view, emphasizing the democratic ethos of pirate gangs and the supposedly equal status of women, Africans, and homosexuals among them. The reality, sadly, had few if any examples of such utopian communities, many more of pirates acting as slave-raiders and as the semi-licensed agents of imperial expansion. Illicit piracy shaded into semi-legitimate 'buccaneering' and officially sanctioned 'privateering' – and social acceptability. Some began and many ended as affluent and respected members of colonial elite society: such were men like Henry Morgan, William Dampier. But if things went wrong, they could always be disavowed and destroyed, as happened in the famous case of William Kidd.

In the late 18th and early 19th centuries, European colonial power suffered severe blows, while Europe itself was embroiled in a series of conflicts unleashed by Franco-British rivalry, the French Revolution, and Napoleon's continental conquests. Spain and Portugal lost most of their colonies – some falling to rival European powers, but most overthrown by revolution among their settler-descended populations. The most important of Britain's American possessions, too, were lost through colonial revolt. Major parts of France's colonial empire were seized by the British during the wars of the 1760s and 1800s; but its most profitable single element, the Caribbean slave colony of Saint Domingue, succumbed to a successful revolution by the enslaved – the only one in history. The very idea of overseas empire seemed to be in retreat, since its long-term consequences for the imperial power seemed so negative. Colonial subjects, it appeared, eventually always demanded the right to self-government. Wealth from empire might produce idleness and decay in the metropolitan economy, as the Spanish example appeared to suggest. It was increasingly doubted whether the transportation and exploitation of African slave labour was economically rational. Some British radicals argued, too, that overseas conquest bred autocratic habits, which then threatened liberty at home. This last was to be a main basis for anti-imperialist sentiment throughout the 19th century.

Even during this era of widespread setbacks for European empire-building, however, colonial expansion continued in parts of Asia, the Pacific, and, to a lesser extent, Africa. Britain was the main beneficiary, with steadily extending control in India, successful settlement colonies in the south Pacific, and an ever-wider scattering of enclaves elsewhere, compensating for the loss of some of her North American holdings. Her merchant shipping, protected

Capt.º James Cook
of the Endeavour.

10. **Imperialists: hero, villain, or god?** When Captain James Cook
first arrived in Hawaii, the inhabitants worshipped him as an
embodiment of their god Lono – or so Cook's shipmates, and numerous
later chroniclers, believed. More recently, though, some scholars have
argued fiercely that the whole story is a typically arrogant piece of
European colonial myth-making. Cook himself, who had risen from
humble origins to become the greatest explorer of his age, was a classic
British imperial hero figure; albeit less warlike than most of the breed.
But the Europeans who followed him into the south Pacific brought
demographic and environmental devastation in their wake.

by an increasingly powerful navy, dominated ever more of the world's long-distance trade. Britain's economy was also growing faster than any other in Europe, and she was the pioneer of many new industrial and agricultural technologies. Historians still debate how much this internal economic development owed to external expansion, to profits from colonial trade and slavery – and vice versa. They also disagree over how far the guiding ideas of this 'second British empire' were those of a modern commercial society – and therefore, in some contemporaries' eyes, not the old-style imperialism at all, but something more benevolent – as opposed to a less contemporary, more aristocratic, and authoritarian set of values. Certainly the belief (or, some would say, the pretence) that Britain had never *intended* to build a global empire became an important part of British rulers' self-image, most famously expressed by the historian J. R. Seeley in the 1880s. They told themselves and others that what they were spreading round the world were the benefits of liberty and of free trade, not the bonds of domination. Yet in India especially, in the Victorian era, British rule came to involve an elaborate ceremonial display of power which owed a lot, again, to ancient Roman models: but also and perhaps ironically, some historians suggest, drew inspiration from Indian traditions of kingship.

From the 1820s onwards the European seaborne empires underwent a new phase of expansion. This accelerated markedly in the last quarter of the 19th century, when most of Africa was very rapidly divided up, and formerly non-colonial powers like Germany, Belgium, and Italy hastily seized vast tracts of land. For the first time an Asian power, Japan, attempted to build a European-type seaborne empire: Japan's empire-building drive was to take on a far more intense and briefly successful form in 1937–45. Much of this 'new imperialism', however, existed at first only on paper, with really effective occupation taking much longer to establish. French administrators in West Africa, as late as the First World War, commented ruefully that they only really controlled the roads – and only so long as their soldiers marched on them.

Well before European powers occupied most of Africa, however, they had already had a profound and devastating impact on the continent through slavery. The Atlantic slave trade is the one part of the seaborne imperial complex which has, rightly, been judged in unequivocally negative terms by all subsequent writers. It also remains probably more ubiquitous in popular memory and cultural evocation than any other historical crime or tragedy except the Nazi Holocaust. Some historians have wondered why this should be so, when – so they would point out – almost all societies in recorded history have involved slavery at some time. We can, however, say, with some confidence that the New World slave systems fed by the Atlantic trade were different from all others – including those within Africa itself – in that they and they alone formed a central, dynamic element in the growth of the modern world. They were unique in their scale and probably in their harshness. They were intertwined with, and depended on, racial ideologies which still poison every society that they affected. They transformed the life of four continents – North and South America, Africa, and Europe.

The total numbers involved remain controversial. Some popular African American writers assert that 150 or 200 million Africans were enslaved or killed, and that any lower estimate is a racist evasion. The probable real total of 12 to 15 million victims is surely terrible enough. A division has also opened up between those who stress the brutality, the sadism, the suffering of Atlantic slavery, and those who emphasize the trade's careful business rationality. The story of slavery from one aspect resembles that of Auschwitz; from another it is part of the history of entrepreneurship. The latter emphasis, if anything, should increase the sense of shame: for it underlines that the trade was not driven by some impersonal state bureaucracy, but by a mass of individual traders making conscious decisions. And although there were Europeans who condemned the enslavement of Africans right from the start, remarkably few of those actively involved seem to have had moral qualms. This further involves re-examination of one of history's great 'chicken and egg' questions: did European beliefs in Africans' natural inferiority come into existence to legitimate their enslavement, or was slavery itself made possible by a prior structure of racist ideas?

Yet the Atlantic trade was not the only one. The empires of south and south-west Asia held and traded slaves on almost the same scale as the European ones. Estimates for the trans-Saharan, Red Sea, and Indian Ocean commerces (together, they are often called 'the Islamic slave trade'; but this is just as dubious as calling the Atlantic one 'Christian') vary very widely. They went on for much longer than the Atlantic slave plunder; and even for the later periods, far fewer written records survive or have been found. Totals, across the centuries, of anything from 3 to 14 million have been suggested, with the most detailed – albeit still admittedly sketchy – calculation being Ralph Austen's of 7,220,000. It was very different in character from the European-dominated enslaving business: slaves were employed more in domestic service and as soldiers, far less as agricultural labourers, than in the New World. It involved far more enslaved women – whether as servants, concubines, or both – than did the latter. Some have argued that 'Islamic' slavery was in the main more humane than European: slaves were not only more typically household members, but might be 'part of the family'. It was easier and more common to buy or be granted one's freedom; ex-slaves or even people whose formal status was still enslaved could rise to high office. Certainly, there were few equivalents in the Islamic world for the vast, brutally exploitative New World plantation systems, or apparently for the hideous rates of mortality which many of these exacted. In the longer term, it is evident that social assimilation of former slaves and their descendants, including intermarriage, has been far more the norm in Islamic societies than in the West. The former had, and have, comparatively little institutionalized racism – to which Islamic teaching is resolutely hostile.

But the balance of moral judgement is fiercely contested. Harsher commentators point out that enslavement of Africans in Islamic societies not only started earlier than in Christian ones, but continued later; that the widespread castration of male slaves was as cruel as anything practised by Americans; and that it was European Christians, not Africans, Asians, or Muslims, who eventually abolished the institution of slavery and forced others to do so. Indeed in the late 19th century, the drive to end the 'Arab slave trade' was offered as a major justification for European colonial expansion in eastern and central Africa: though there was undoubtedly much hypocrisy and self-deception in claims that this was its main motivation.

All the colonial powers in Africa, in varying degrees and different ways, connived at the perpetuation of indigenous slave systems. Even where they acted with some decisiveness to abolish trading in slaves, as the British did in most (though not all) of their colonies, their general stance towards African domestic slavery was to encourage its gradual erosion by cautious alterations in legal and tax codes, not to outlaw it outright. The latter course, it was felt, would create too much disruption and resistance, especially from the local rulers on whose cooperation Indirect Rule systems depended. And in some cases, colonial rulers' implication in slavery went considerably further. In French central North Africa and British-ruled Sudan, colonial armies were in large part composed of slaves, just as those of precolonial states had been; though European commanders professed pious ignorance of this fact. Forced labour conscription – routine throughout colonized Africa and almost throughout the years of European rule, but especially intense and brutal during the First World War – often seemed hard to distinguish from outright enslavement. And in places like French Mauritania, large-scale local slave-owning persisted right through the colonial era – and beyond. Perhaps the most poignant expression of this continued European colonial embroilment in African slavery was the case of Arthur Rimbaud. The brilliant young poet whose precocious teenage writings had celebrated the boundless spirit of freedom abandoned literature and went to Africa; in search of adventure, romance – and wealth. There, the great rhapsodist of liberty certainly owned, and probably bought and sold, domestic slaves.

The slave trade was not, even so, the most devastating aspect of the rise of the seaborne empires. Another, still more dramatic and far-reaching consequence of Europeans' global outreach was ecological. Plants and animals as well as people were carried across the oceans, transforming the ecological balances, the economies, and the landscapes of the entire world – though most rapidly and sweepingly those of the neo-Europes where large numbers of settlers clustered. Yet it was not large domestic mammals or food plants whose immediate impact was greatest, but organisms which could not be seen, and whose very existence was long entirely unknown. European ships and the people they carried brought previously unknown diseases to the Americas and the Pacific.

Thus the initial demographic impact of European colonialism was devastatingly negative: indigenous populations throughout the New World and on many Pacific islands were reduced to a fraction of their former numbers, or entirely wiped out. In parts of Africa, too, the collision with Europe produced demographic catastrophe: it has been estimated, for instance, that the population of the Belgian Congo diminished by nine or ten million in the decades following conquest. In the longer run, however, for those colonized peoples who survived this initial 'fatal impact', the trend was often reversed. Infant mortality rates dropped sharply, life expectancy increased, some previously endemic diseases were controlled or eradicated, and much of the non-European world began to emulate the 'population explosion' which Europe had experienced much earlier. All this was substantially attributable, of course, to the introduction of Western medical techniques to the colonies: though it should be remembered that this 'European' medical knowledge in its turn owed much to Chinese, Indian, Arab, and other 'Asian' discoveries.

In between, there were vast but half-forgotten disasters; most notably, the 'El Niño famines' of the late-Victorian era. First in 1876–9, then again in 1896–1900, huge swathes of India, northern China, and Brazil were devastated. At least 30 million, perhaps as many as 60 million, people died in those countries alone. And lesser but still murderous crop failures, with ensuing starvation, hit many other parts of the tropics and south in the same period – from Java to southern Africa, Korea to the Sudan and Ethiopia. The total global death toll can only be guessed at; but was almost certainly greater than for any other disaster in recorded history, except perhaps the Black Death.

The immediate cause of the disasters was 'El Niño' (the Christ Child): a periodic over-heating of the southern Pacific which, in a pattern only discovered in the late 1960s, produces a potentially disastrous complex of side effects including failure of the monsoon rains across the tropics and beyond. Nature's fury, though, produced indeed only *potential* disaster. As always, it was human action and inaction that turned dangerous possibility into hideous actuality. As Amartya Sen was the first to show, people very rarely suffer and die simply because there isn't enough food to go round. When shortages strike, it is economic structures, social networks, and political decisions that produce famine, that determine who will die, and how many they will be. In the short run, people died in their millions not just because their crops failed, but because their rulers were incompetent, uncaring, and, in many of the worst-affected countries, suffused with racist colonial contempt for, and indifference towards, their suffering subjects. But broader, structural forces were at work too. As the great powers of the day – with Britain still at their head – completed the carving up of the globe into both actual colonies and (as in China) less formalized spheres of influence, they also cemented in place a new world financial system and a new international division of labour. One facet of this was that many parts of the non-European world, previously self-sufficient in basic foods, were now forced into being suppliers of cheap raw materials for the rich countries. Their governments, whether these were mere colonial appointees or nominally

11. **Collaborators:** Indian officer, 2nd Regiment Bengal Irregular Cavalry, 1852. British rule in India rested ultimately on military force; but even after the 'Mutiny' of 1857, that force was mainly composed of Indians. Unlike many colonial armies, those of the East India Company and the Raj had native officers as well as soldiers – though senior positions remained in entirely British hands. This man's regiment had a long and chequered career. It was first raised in 1809 by William Gardner, who had previously fought as a mercenary with the forces of two Indian princes. Its successor, Gardner's Horse, still exists today as part of the modern Indian Army.

independent, indigenous rulers, would not or dared not follow policies – like large-scale famine relief – which challenged that new world order. Some, indeed, grasped at the devastation wrought by famine as an opportunity to expand or consolidate their power.

More broadly, these disasters were part of the process that produced the 'Third World': the vast gulf between rich and poor, developed and underdeveloped, which took form in the later 19th century, which had no real precedent in human history, and which not only persists, but by many measures continues to widen, today. It remains, again, controversial how far that huge division between rich and poor on a global scale should be attributed to the existence of the European empires. Some analysts argue strongly that the European powers (and later the United States) systematically created underdevelopment in the rest of the world, and that colonial policies were deliberately directed to that end. Others suggest that the relation of cause and effect ran more the other way around: that it was the imbalance between relative European wealth, state power, and perhaps above all superior technology – an imbalance already evident well before the colonial empires reached their zenith – which made modern colonialism possible, far more than vice versa. In one version of this latter argument – perhaps most forcefully expressed by the late Ernest Gellner – empire as such was relatively unimportant, compared to the far greater economic and scientific transformations of which it was, in large part, a mere temporary consequence.

Others still would question whether modern imperialism can or should be evaluated at such a level of generality, because it was so radically diverse in different places. For instance, was there, in any real sense, a singular 'British empire' at any one time, let alone across time (for historians often refer to the 'First', 'Second', 'Third', and sometimes even more British empires in chronological succession)? At their greatest extent just after the 1914–18 war, Britain's overseas possessions included Crown Colonies (mostly without significant European-descended populations) across

Africa, the Caribbean, and south-east Asia, self-governing Dominions mainly inhabited by people of British or other European ancestry, numerous islands and enclaves around the globe held mainly as strategic bases, like Malta, Aden, Gibraltar, and Singapore, former Turkish and German colonies held under various kinds of League of Nations Mandatory authority, the vast Indian territories, which were in themselves an extraordinarily complex patchwork of forms of rule, and so on. France's empire was of course somewhat smaller, and was ruled (supposedly) in a more centralizing, rationalist spirit, but was in reality only a little less diverse.

It may be possible, all the same, to see all these different colonized places and their forms of rule as falling into a few broad categories. The most fundamental division was perhaps that between settlement and non-settlement colonies. The first kind were, obviously enough, those places where large numbers of Europeans moved and remained. In some – the 'neo-Europes' – they became the vast majority; in others, like Algeria, South Africa, and more precariously in Kenya or Zimbabwe, they were dominant minorities. Most of these migrants came from the imperial 'mother countries', among which Britain was by far the most successful creator of settlement colonies, and depended on those countries for military protection. But there were others too: the Dutch in southern Africa, many non-French southern Europeans in Algeria, very large numbers of Irish in all Britain's possessions, surprising numbers of Germans all over the place, and more. The motivation for settlement was overwhelmingly economic. Migrants searched for cheap or free land, often for cheap native labour, or for better-paid employment – not all settlers were farmers, or wanted to be. Indeed several of these new societies, like Australia, were heavily urbanized from an early date. Some, though, sought to escape religious or political persecution in the 'old country', or at least to continue ways of life which were felt to be under threat there. There was thus quite a strong drive among colonists to transplant the habits of their homelands wholesale and even impose them on others. British settlers, perhaps especially, tried to maintain the customs and manners they had known in the old world, in every essential sphere of life from food and clothing to architecture and town planning – even where adapting indigenous ways might have been thought to be far more rational.

Yet a sense of being different from the 'old country', having distinct and sometimes conflicting interests from those of its rulers, eventually feeling oppressed by it and demanding self-rule, grew up almost everywhere. In some cases – most obviously among white minorities in Africa – this meant mainly that the settlers wanted to maintain more extreme racial inequalities than the mother-country government found acceptable. In others, the push for self-government had more respectable democratic credentials. In the Americas (leaving aside the anomalous cases of the Caribbean societies where descendants of African slaves and/or Asian indentured labourers were the majority) and the Pacific, every settler colony succeeded in becoming politically independent. Almost all of them achieved this well before any of the non-settler territories did so. In Africa, by contrast, no settler community managed to gain and keep power – with South Africa's 1990s transition marking the end of the last attempt at it. Yet in Africa too, settlers' long efforts to achieve self-government under their own minority rule produced almost all the significant violence in post-1945 decolonization. Those efforts delayed, deflected, or thwarted the European decolonizing powers' plans, as well as those of African nationalist movements. And in almost every case, with Algeria the great exception, such communities succeeded in maintaining much of their economic and even some of their political predominance after independence.

It could rather ironically be argued, then, that white settler communities challenged the power of empire far more successfully and earlier than almost any of the empires' conquered peoples could do. Colonial powers were usually unwilling to resort to physical repression against settlers as they did against non-European peoples. Imperial conflicts against rebellious whites were rarely on anything near the same scale as those in India or black Africa – with the sole exception of the 1899 Anglo-Boer War. Often they were little more than glorified police operations against small and ill-armed settler groups who may have intended protest at misgovernment, rather than revolution. Such were the French-Canadian rising of 1837–8, the affair of the Eureka Stockade in Australia in 1854, and Riel's Canadian revolt of 1885, largely backed by indigenous and mixed-descent hunters, fur traders, and trappers. In the era of decolonization, I cannot think of any instance where the armed forces of the metropolitan power were used in armed combat against rebellious white settlers, with a few very marginal Algerian exceptions. Britain found it politically unacceptable to deploy troops against Rhodesian whites when they unilaterally and illegally declared their independence in the 1960s.

The non-settler colonies – colonies of occupation, or of exploitation, as some historians would call them – were considerably more numerous and far more disparate in nature. Across such vast diversity, generalizations about their character are fraught with difficulty. Nonetheless, many more or less bold, more or less influential attempts have been made at such generalization. Let us look briefly at three especially important areas where this has been done: in relation to the economics of empire, to the ideologies and cultural practices of the empire builders, and the responses of the colonized.

Economies

The economic balance sheet of colonialism, for both imperialist and colonized countries, presents a hugely complex, mixed record: one over which economic historians have long disputed, and will continue to do so. We saw that in the ancient, and the more modern, land empires tax revenues, tribute, or simple plunder flowed from the subject territories to the imperial centres. Yet this did not necessarily involve a systematic impoverishment of the peripheries and enrichment of the centre. Anatolia remained among the

> The most important result of colonization is to increase world productivity. It is at the same time a great social force for progress. The earth belongs to humanity. It belongs to those who know best how to develop it, increase its wealth, and in the process augment it, beautify it and elevate humanity. Colonization is the propagation of the highest form of civilization yet conceived and realized, the perpetuation of the most talented race, the progressive organization of humanity.
>
> **Georges Deherme, 1908.**
>
> (Quoted in Alice L. Conklin, *A Mission to Civilize* (Stanford, Calif., 1997), p. 55)

poorest parts of the Ottoman empire, and it would have been hard to convince 19th-century Russian peasants – or their descendants today – that they gained any economic benefit from ruling over Uzbeks or Estonians.

Many writers have believed, however, that the modern European empires *did* involve such a systematic robbing of colonies to enrich the metropole. That, it was insisted, was what colonial empires were *for*, their reason for being. This in turn was because, unlike their precursors, the modern empires were distinctively capitalist creations, founded, shaped, and driven by the profit motive. A vast literature has developed debating such views. It is impossible to summarize or evaluate that debate here. Instead, we shall briefly sketch the 'negative' and 'positive' views of the economic effects of empire – perhaps in rather extreme forms.

The negative assessment says that African, Asian, and other precolonial economies were developing independently before the coming of European rule, and there is no reason to think that they

would not have continued to do so. In some, indeed, all the
preconditions for future commercial and industrial dynamism were
present, as in India with its huge production of textiles. Colonial
rule destroyed these conditions where they existed, and blocked the
possibility of their emerging elsewhere. Colonized areas were forced
into acting as sources of underpriced raw materials for European
industry and of cheap, often forced or enslaved, labour. They were
not allowed to develop industries of their own, except in the few
cases where this suited European needs. Any profits were not
reinvested within the colonies, but repatriated by the rulers. The
same went for colonial taxes and other state revenues, except where
these were spent – as most in fact were – on soldiers and police,
which meant forcing the colonized to pay for their own subjugation.
Where there was not savage exploitation, there was utter neglect:
colonial governments spent almost nothing on education, health
care, social welfare, or infrastructure; except when, near the very
end of the colonial era, they were forced to do so by political
pressures.

The net result was the 'development of underdevelopment', leaving
almost all ex-colonial societies and their newly independent
governments to face extreme poverty with few resources, little
domestic industry, and low levels of 'human capital' in skills and
education. Their economies were heavily dependent on grossly
unequal external links rather than being self-reliant. And since the
end of colonial rule, that pattern has often been perpetuated, with
multinational companies and financial institutions carrying on
where the colonial rulers left off.

The positive case argues that, on the contrary, colonialism played
an economically progressive role. Colonial rule was the means by
which European technology, culture, and institutions – the things
which had enabled Europe itself to develop and industrialize –
were spread across the rest of the world. Under this influence,
almost all colonized areas developed more rapidly than they
would have done if they had remained independent. Empire was

12. Selling Empire: 'Buy Empire Goods from Home and Overseas': a British Empire Marketing Board advertisement, c.1930.

mutually beneficial. At worst, it was the lesser of two evils facing non-European societies. The likely alternative to imperial rule was not independent development, but anarchy or stagnation. Colonial overlords generally provided more efficient and honest government than the precolonial states had done. Empires were not engines of exploitation, but of modernization. Imperial metropoles – especially Britain – provided bigger and better markets for colonial products than they could otherwise have found. As to postcolonial economic failures, these do not result mainly from the colonial legacy or the malevolence of international capitalism. They are first and foremost the responsibility of indigenous postcolonial governments and elites; their incompetence, greed, brutality, or captivation by economically disastrous ideologies like Marxism. The rapid growth of Singapore's or (on an entirely different scale) India's economies shows that the colonial legacy need be no barrier to prosperity. The extreme poverty of Ethiopia indicates that largely escaping colonial rule is no guarantee of success.

It hardly needs saying that neither of these polarized arguments is convincing as a *global* picture of the economic effects of empire. Colonial economies were simply too diverse for one account to fit all. In some places, the colonial impact totally transformed economic conditions. In others, it merely continued or intensified trends which already existed. In the first category would obviously fall those places, like Australia and all of the Americas, which had apparently had no pre-existing economic interaction with the rest of the world. It would also include colonies of large-scale settlement. Empire was, on the whole, economically a very good thing for white settlers. They were, in fact, in many ways its clearest beneficiaries. White communities in the main British settlement colonies – the United States, Canada, Australia, New Zealand but also settlers in Africa and parts of the Caribbean – rapidly became the most prosperous societies in the 19th- and early 20th-century world. Modern attempts to ascertain profit and loss from Britain's colonial empire have reached differing and often agnostic conclusions about empire's economic value to Britain itself. Where they have almost all agreed, however, is that British imperial settler communities were net beneficiaries, on a huge scale – not least because their defence costs were largely borne by Britain. This was in extreme contrast to non-settlement colonies, where military expenditure swallowed up almost uniquely high proportions of local revenues. In fairness one should add that several of these societies, notably Australia and New Zealand, also had some of the world's most egalitarian income distributions, and some of the world's earliest full electoral democracies. And some European-settled postcolonies had less happy experiences. The strangest case here is perhaps Argentina. In the 19th and early 20th centuries it was growing and industrializing at least as dynamically as the USA or Australia. Thereafter it told a far gloomier story; and indeed at the time of writing (early 2002) the country faces total economic collapse.

In other places the colonial economic impact was less all-embracing and more open to dispute. In parts of Africa, especially the most remote rural areas, colonial rule had only a minimal direct economic effect, except for sometimes rather desultory attempts to impose taxes on people who had not previously used money. The need to obtain cash to pay tax did change economic life by forcing some people into cash-crop production or migrant labour. But in many such areas, wider economic transformations only really began near the end of the colonial era – when European rulers began to pursue far more activist policies, which have been called a 'second colonial occupation' – or even after. In some African regions, though, it is of course likely that the greatest and most damaging European economic influences came well before the establishment of formal colonial rule, with the effects of the slave trade. And in others again, colonial economic change cut far deeper, earlier. This was most powerfully true of South Africa, with the successive comings of commercial agriculture (African attempts to compete with settlers in this were deliberately quashed by government), mining, industrialization, and a racially segregated labour market.

In British India, too, colonialism's economic effects remain much disputed. Early nationalist economic historians believed that indigenous industry was deliberately destroyed by the British. But some other scholars argue that the economic influence of state policies or of British capitalists should not be exaggerated: Indian entrepreneurs, industries, and trading networks retained a great deal of wealth and power. Colonialism as such, in this interpretation, is not necessarily the most important fact about a colonial economy. Local activity and initiative – including indigenous class interests and conflicts – should be given their due. It follows that neither the advent of colonial control, nor its end, was necessarily a crucial economic watershed. This kind of view has, however, been attacked in its turn for supposedly passing the buck from British to Indians, even 'blaming the victim' for Indian problems. Some fairly ill-tempered exchanges have ensued.

Some effects are not doubted. The global seaborne empires were evidently crucial in shaping the modern world's networks of long-distance trade, though in some places they merely built on or took over ones in which Chinese, Indian, Arab, and other non-European merchants had long been engaged. Startlingly, the first truly globalized imperial commodities were almost all drugs: coffee and tea, tobacco and opium, alcoholic drinks, and the more quietly addictive sugar and chocolate. Many of them were produced by slave labour. But over time, the variety and the volume of goods involved increased exponentially. Neither the existence nor even the scale of contemporary globalization of trade is at all novel. For centuries, though, global trade was in large part trade within empires – with a consistent broad pattern of Europe (and later the neo-Europes) importing raw materials, exporting manufactures.

World financial and monetary integration too was forged by empire. Colonial rule forced the use of money on places – especially in Africa and the Americas – which had previously managed without. It spread the use of its own currencies, or tied others to them. British imperial power depended heavily on sterling's position as a

> And it was at this moment, as I stood there with the rifle in my hands, that I first grasped the hollowness, the futility of the white man's dominion in the East. Here was I, the white man with his gun, standing in front of the unarmed native crowd – seemingly the leading actor in the piece; but in reality I was only an absurd puppet pushed to and fro by the will of those yellow faces behind. I perceived in this moment that when the white man turns tyrant it is his own freedom that he destroys. He becomes a sort of hollow, posturing dummy, the conventionalized figure of a sahib. For it is a condition of his rule that he shall spend his life in trying to impress the 'natives' and so in every crisis he has got to do what the 'natives' expect of him. He wears a mask, and his face grows to fit it.
>
> George Orwell, 'Shooting an Elephant' 1936
>
> (*Collected Essays, Journalism and Letters* (Harmondsworth, 1970), i. 269)

world currency – and vice versa. France in a sense went further, introducing a single currency throughout its empire; many former French colonies still remain effectively tied to it today.

Ideologies and Cultures

Empire depended on a belief in superiority, and on arguments vindicating that belief. It is possible that some ancient imperialists felt no need to justify themselves: that they were perfectly happy to conquer and rule over others simply because they *could*, with no ideology beyond the assertion that Might makes Right. The royal art of the Assyrians looks to some viewers as though that was very much their attitude. The rulers of every major empire at least since the Romans, however, offered arguments and justifications for what they did. The starting point for such arguments was always that there was some essential difference between them and those they subjected to their rule.

Ideas of this kind were, naturally, almost universal *within* particular societies: those who ruled were entitled to do so by their superior wisdom, intelligence, virtue, godliness, or even (in the argument of the 18th-century philosopher Edmund Burke) just because, having been brought up and trained in the habits of rule, they could do so with greater skill and moderation than people without such training. Many of the arguments used to justify colonial rule were carried over directly from such domestic contexts. It has often been pointed out, for instance, how closely many 19th-century European contentions about supposedly inferior or degenerate non-white races resembled older claims about the labouring poor within Britain, France, or Spain. Despite this, colonialist claims to superiority as justification for rule took specific forms – indeed a whole elaborate repertoire of them.

The most powerful and widespread early-modern argument vindicating empire was a religious one. This was the dominant propaganda theme – and no doubt often the genuinely dominant preoccupation – of Spanish and Portuguese expansion in the 16th century, and featured heavily in other, slightly later British, French, and other imperial ideologies too. It looked back to the ideas of the Crusades against Muslims and other 'heathens', and to medieval and late Roman notions of the Church as universal *imperium*. Christians, bearing knowledge of the only true religion, had not only a right but a God-given duty to carry it to the rest of humanity. But this impulse was given new inflections, and a new urgency, by the conflicts within Europe that followed the Protestant Reformation. Not only should new worlds be won for Christendom, but specifically for one's own particular version of it, denying opportunities of conquest and conversion to the heretics.

The religious case for empire-building, however, could point in radically different directions in terms of colonial policy. On one side, it implied that the main purpose of colonial rule was to convert the 'natives', which of course implied educating them in Christian doctrine and behaving decently towards them: even, after conversion, treating them as equals, 'Brothers and Sisters in Christ'. On the other side lay the idea that infidels – especially if they had been offered the chance of conversion and had refused it – were naturally wicked and depraved, and might well have no rights that a Christian need respect. They could be subjugated, exploited, or even exterminated with a clear conscience. This posed especial dilemmas for colonial slave-owners. Their religious duty, it was widely held, was to Christianize their slaves. But if they did so, a common bond of humanity between them had to be recognized, transcending and perhaps challenging the division between master and chattel. And as we shall see, religious arguments could also be and increasingly were deployed *against* empire, as well as against slavery.

Overarching the religious justifications for empire, and to some extent replacing them over time, were cultural – or civilizational – ones. The superiority of Europeans, and thus their right to rule others, was established by their supposedly far greater achievements in inventiveness, control over nature, their construction of elaborate political, economic, artistic, and intellectual structures. The allegedly huge gulf between Europeans and others was explained in various ways. Environment and climate might account for it: tropical conditions were widely held to induce physical and mental weakness or idleness, which led to their inhabitants' supposedly low levels of cultural achievement. An unwelcome by-product of this belief was obsessive anxiety that too much sun might cause degeneracy among Europeans in the tropics too. That's why, in old photographs, they can usually be seen wearing far too many clothes for the climate.

The inferiority of the colonized might, of course, be seen as the product of historical circumstances, implying that under different conditions non-Europeans could achieve just as much as whites believed they did. It followed that the purpose and justification of empire was to create those conditions among the colonized: it was essentially an educational or civilizing enterprise. Or it might be that differences in culture or technological achievement reflected biological ones. Humanity was sharply and unalterably divided into 'racial' groups, arranged in a clear hierarchy of superiority and inferiority. European whites were at the top of this pyramid or ladder, and only they were fully capable of abstract thought, technical progress, efficient government, true cultural creativity, and so on. In many versions, more specifically, *northern* Europeans, sometimes called 'Aryan' or 'Nordic', or particular nationalities like the English or Germans, were at the top. Many Asian peoples occupied intermediate positions. Some were acknowledged to possess considerable intelligence, and Indian, Chinese, or Arab civilizational achievements could not be entirely denied. But they were widely believed to possess profound flaws in their collective character, being congenitally dissolute, idle, dishonest, cruel, and so on. An influential current in modern writing about empire, most eloquently formulated by Edward W. Said, labels this structure of European ideas about Asians 'Orientalism' and argues that it remains alive and well today.

Africans were lower still down the scale, often believed to be inherently less intelligent and incapable of building or sustaining an 'advanced' civilization. One current of 19th-century European thought – though a minority one – even doubted whether Africans were fully human. Other schools of colonialist opinion obsessively catalogued and categorized different African groups according to their supposedly varying levels of intelligence and their potential to become civilized. Often, the 'better' groups were suggested to have some distant trace of non-African ancestry, which accounted for their higher status.

At the very bottom of this hierarchy of human groups lay the native peoples of the Americas and the south Pacific, with Aboriginal Australians perhaps the most despised of all. Many European thinkers believed that these were not only at the lowest level of primitivism, but were inevitably doomed to extinction. It was not, most such thinkers protested, that they *wanted* this to happen. It was simply a law of nature that when higher groups came into contact with lower ones, the latter would gradually disappear from the earth, just as animal species did when they could not adapt to changed environments.

There is much dispute over the age and ancestry of ideas like these. Some authorities argue that racialized thought is a very modern and very European invention. Others say that it can clearly be found in the ancient world, and among many non-European peoples. There is little doubt, though, that such thought became *dominant* among European rulers and thinkers, became a major rationalization for empire, and massively influenced all aspects of colonial policy, during the later 19th century. During this period, it was generally believed that the existence of racial divisions and hierarchies was proved by science. That belief was steadily undermined during the 20th century, while the experience of fascism seemed to discredit the *explicit* basing of state policies on ideas about race, in the colonial world as elsewhere. Late colonialism increasingly shifted – or shifted back – to self-justifications in terms of cultural difference. Sometimes, this seemed to be just a change of language, not of underlying attitudes. But it meant that colonial authorities, more and more, had to abandon assertions of a simple, straightforward right to rule, and argue instead that they were acting as 'trustees' on behalf of those still incapable of running their own affairs, and indeed on behalf of humanity as a whole. This meant they had to be seen to be pursuing policies of development, education, and welfare for the benefit of the colonized, and even preparing them for eventual self-government.

The idea of self-rule for the European empires' subject peoples, however, was not widely believed in – at least among Europeans themselves – until very late in the day. There were always critics of empire among the imperial powers' own people, including some who wanted to see the entire system of colonial rule dismantled immediately. But they were nearly always small, dissident minorities. Opposition to colonial expansion stemmed (to cut a complex story brutally short) largely from pragmatic considerations: that it was economically purposeless or, in France after 1871, a wasteful distraction from the recovery of Alsace-Lorraine. Or it was opposed out of fears that expansion overseas strengthened the forces of autocracy at home: this argument was the mainstay of British liberal anti-imperialists throughout the 19th century, and of German and Belgian critics at the century's end. There was some humanitarian concern for the victims of colonial conquest; but this was fitful and unorganized, a concern of (usually religious) minorities. And, as with the sentimental British cult of Zulu monarch Cetshwayo or the French one of West African warlord Samori Toure, it was mostly expressed only when the former enemy was safely dead or captive. After Britain's defeat of the Sudanese Mahdist revolt in 1898, Radicals, churchmen, and even Queen Victoria herself protested at Kitchener's desecration of the Mahdi's bones; but hardly anyone in Britain spoke up for him when he was alive. There was more vocal opposition within Britain to the 1899 Anglo-Boer War – but this had much to do with the fact that unusually for a colonial war, the adversaries were white.

Anticolonialism in the strong sense – the politico-moral condemnation of all colonial conquest, demands for the rapid abandonment of all colonial possessions, belief in a universal right to national self-determination – was the preserve of tiny minorities in Britain, France, or any other colonialist power before about the 1920s. It was not, contrary to much subsequent myth-making, the belief of most early socialists or indeed Marxists. Marx himself had regarded British rule in India as historically progressive despite its brutalities. He and Engels saw most colonized peoples as falling into the category which they, following Hegel, dismissed as 'non-historical'; groups which, no longer capable of an independent existence, are inevitably absorbed by the larger nations.

> England, it is true, in causing a social revolution in Hindustan was actuated only by the vilest interests, and was stupid in her manner of enforcing them. But that is not the question. The question is, can mankind fulfil its destiny without a fundamental revolution in the social state of Asia? If not, whatever may have been the crimes of England she was the unconscious tool of history in bringing about that revolution.
>
> Karl Marx, 'The British Rule in India' (1853)

Empire was often justified in religious terms. Yet religious figures were also among the earliest critics of empire from within Europe. Bartolome de Las Casas, the Spanish bishop who already in the 1540s demanded an end to his country's oppression of the native South Americans, has been called the first European anticolonialist. Later, colonial mission activity involved sharp critiques of imperial policies, exploitation, and racism, as well as enthusiastic complicity in those things. The roles of various Nonconformist and Evangelical groups in anti-slavery agitation, of missions (especially Baptists) in Caribbean anticolonial protest, and of many Christian bodies in opposition to white minority rule in southern Africa, were all substantial. Much of this is unsurprising, and not only because most modern understandings of the ethical values implied by Christianity – and other major world faiths – take these to be opposed to all forms of exploitation, but for more pragmatic reasons. Missionaries, after all, did not usually have direct economic or political motivations for engaging in colonial projects. Their activities were more fully and purely directed towards cultural and psychological change than any other actors on colonial stages. And they were, on the whole, seeking explicitly to transform the consciousness of colonized subjects; whereas for governments and administrators (especially under Indirect Rule systems) such transformation was either peripheral and secondary, or even something deliberately to be avoided as a potentially destabilizing, unmanageable kind of interference. In many colonial situations, moreover, missionaries might be the only locally based whites (not that colonial missions *were* all white, as is often carelessly assumed) from relatively humble backgrounds, the only ones living in intimate daily contact with colonized populations, and the only ones trying to provide education or health care to them. There was, though, something of a paradox here. Missionaries often stood at a distance from the political and economic imperatives of colonial rule, and even in opposition to them. But in many of their activities – religious conversion itself, spreading European-style education, pressing their own ideas of morality, family life, and social customs on their followers – they might be seen by critics as the most active and intrusive of all the forces of cultural imperialism.

Such paradoxes, apparent inconsistencies, and divergent trends marked almost all aspects of colonial ideology. Colonial rule was widely presented and understood as a great modernizing force. Yet it contained backward-looking, and even antiquarian, impulses too. If one historian, Gauri Viswanathan, has seen British India as the first testing-ground of modern education systems, then another, Raphael Samuel, finds there one of the birthplaces of the heritage industry, and 'one of the great laboratories in which conservationist practices were developed'. In Africa, British administrators' affinity for traditional rulers – especially, as in northern Nigeria, where these had all the trappings of a medieval or feudal exoticism – was matched by disdain for the 'educated African', the obstreperous man of superficial but unwelcome modernity, akin both to the similarly despised Bengali 'Babu' and to the 'barrack-room lawyer' at home. A 'myth of Merrie Africa' was fostered with assiduity, an ideal of timeless village community as appealing to radicals and socialists as to conservatives. Imperial Britain proclaimed itself as a democracy at home, yet conferred only subjecthood, not citizenship, on its colonial subjects. But then, Britain's domestic political system was never, during the centuries of her rule over India, a 'full' democracy either; the legal titles and rights of citizenship existed no more in Manchester than in Madras. Colonial rule, in denying

13. Imperialists: The empire builder as mystic. Pierre Savorgnon de Brazza. Less ferocious and materialistic than many European pioneers in Africa, Brazza seems genuinely to have loved Africa, and to have seen exploration as an end in itself. Yet he, more than any other single person, was responsible for establishing France's often brutal rule in large parts of central Africa.

democracy, seemed to negate any concept of the state's duty to its subjects. Yet the rhetoric of responsibility, however one-sided or hypocritical, was one of the most ubiquitous features of the Raj and many other colonial regimes, especially in their later years.

One of the most constantly repeated tropes in the literature of empire was that of Fate: it was foredestined that European civilization should find itself having to clash with those who resisted its onward march. But this coexisted with an often bitter hostility to that very 'advance of civilization' – for British imperial romancers like Henry Rider Haggard, John Buchan, and Rudyard Kipling, the excitement of empire came precisely from its possibilities of escaping the stifling embrace of civilized places and values. The idea of the noble savage died hard: novelists and poets like these were passionate in their admiration for the most 'untamed' of native peoples, like the Zulu, or the Pathans of the North-West Frontier. The theme was echoed even by writers from European countries without colonies, like the popular Polish novelist Henryk Sienkiewicz.

The late-Victorian propaganda of empire did not only stress modernization, but standardly depicted its pioneers – explorers, soldiers, missionaries, frontiersmen – as paragons of rationality, maturity, and self-control, in stark contrast to the wild, unruly, often childlike peoples they met and dominated. Anticolonialist literature, seeing such figures by contrast as brutal exploiters, nonetheless concurs in portraying them as masterful and rational. Yet many among these pioneers of empire in its last phase of growth more resemble the pirates and buccaneers who operated on empire's fringes in an earlier age: like the neurotic but brutal fantasist Henry Morton Stanley or the sadistic Carl Peters. And in contrast to both deifying and demonizing portrayals of such men, another historian has recently documented how many of them seem to have been not only permanently bemused by what they encountered, but often drunk, drug-addicted, or mentally unbalanced.

It was, or seemed to be, a man's world. And that too was doubtless part of the appeal to many would-be imperialists: empire as a vast outdoor extension of the gentleman's club, officers' mess, or masonic lodge, or indeed as an open field for predatory male sexuality, both hetero- and homosexual. It is true that there were usually few European women in non-settler colonies, and that the theorists, publicists, and artists of empire were almost as overwhelmingly male as were its rulers. There was a strong tradition of rhetoric and imagery by which imperialists identified themselves and their mission with masculine virtues, and the colonized with feminine weakness and dependency. Yet women's roles in imperialism too were complex, paradoxical – and much disputed among modern historians. Some argue that early Western feminism was itself colonialist: it made its bid for women's equality only by, and through, assertions of inter-gender racial partnership in a colonial mission. The women writers of empire, for instance, were no more capable of true dialogue with the colonized than were men. Other modern critics, though, emphasize how some European women were early and courageous critics of imperialism; while the anti-slavery campaigns in several countries were probably the first modern political movements anywhere to involve mass female participation. Some women writers drew sympathetic parallels between racial inequality in the colonies and domestic gender divisions. And it is often pointed out – perhaps a little self-righteously – that European women cannot be blamed for the crimes or follies of empire, since they had no real share of power in it.

Colonial impacts and contacts, and their cultural representations, were as various, and often as internally complex and contradictory, as the societies, social groups, and indeed individuals they brought together. For every celebration of difference between rulers and ruled, we can find an insistent search for similarities. For every assertion of civilizational superiority on one side, we can see counter-assertions making similar claims from the other. If some empire builders used the rhetoric of modernization and a civilizing mission, others found in colonial conflicts precisely the evidence they wanted that a primal, desired barbarism still flowed in English, or French, or German bloodstreams. Some thought the main aim of empire was cultural assimilation: making 'them' just like 'us'. Others believed that idea was impossible – or were horrified by it. If imperialism depended, as Joseph Conrad famously asserted, on a redeeming idea, then there was not just one idea, but a whole mass of contradictory, clashing ones.

> The conquest of the earth, which mostly means the taking it away from those who have a different complexion or slightly flatter noses than ourselves, is not a pretty thing when you look into it too much. What redeems it is the idea only. An idea at the back of it; not a sentimental pretence but an idea; and an unselfish belief in the idea – something you can set up, and bow down before, and offer a sacrifice to.
>
> **Joseph Conrad, *Heart of Darkness* (1899)**

Resistance, collaboration, and adaptation

Colonial conquest met resistance almost everywhere; which is as we would expect. But such resistance was almost always ineffective and unsuccessful; which requires a little more explanation. Much emphasis has been, and indeed should be, placed on disparities in military technology. These grew wider with time, especially by the later 19th century when European armies had repeating rifles, breech-loading, rifled cannon, machine guns, and armoured steamships. But organizational and cultural differences may have been at least as important. The conquering forces were often much smaller than their adversaries, but they were usually professional, with a unified, centralized command structure and strict combat discipline. None of these necessarily applied to the resistance. In fact European invaders were very often able to exploit division and disunity among their opponents. In most cases, they could recruit the bulk of their fighting men from among the colonized populations themselves. If Africans or Indians had united against the colonialists, then colonization would have been impossible, except at staggering, unacceptable human and financial cost. But to do that, they would have had to think of themselves *as* 'Africans' or 'Indians', a single people with shared interests, in the first place. Before the 20th century, very few could even potentially do so.

As it was, colonial conquest was usually relatively cheap – at least in terms of European lives. It was almost never comparable in human cost, on the *colonizers'* side, to major European or North American wars of the time. Even where European armies were defeated, as at Adowa, Isandhlwana, or Maiwand, or where victory was won only after bloodbaths like Ferozeshah and Chilianwalla in Britain's Sikh wars, these cost considerably fewer European lives than did the great intra-European battles of the 18th or 19th, let alone the 20th, centuries. On the other side, the human cost of colonial conquest was often vastly greater, in both absolute and relative terms – even if we think only in purely military terms, leaving aside the death tolls from disease, famine, enslavement, and other evils which empire often brought in its train. This was certainly not only the case in the big, well-known imperial wars. For instance, the almost entirely forgotten Volta-Bani rebellion against French rule in 1915–16 has been estimated to have cost 30,000 African lives – more dead than Britain lost on the first day of the Somme, or America in the Normandy battles after D-Day.

Alongside all the colonial rhetoric of a 'civilizing mission' – which was certainly not always hollow or insincere – colonial rule might involve immense savagery, especially at its first imposition. It was generally accepted that different rules applied when fighting 'savages' than in warfare between European powers. Prisoners and the wounded were routinely massacred, by British as well as other colonial armies. During an African rebellion in what is now Zimbabwe one settler-soldier, W. A. Jarvis, wrote: 'Our plan of

14. Colonial war staged as big-game hunting. British South Africa Company troops posing with Ndebele dead from 1896 uprising. Such barbaric images would never have been published if they came from a war against fellow Europeans.

campaign will probably be to proceed against this lot and wipe them out, then move on towards Bulawayo wiping out every nigger and every kraal we can find . . . after these cold-blooded murders you may be sure there will be no quarter and everything black will have to die, for our men's blood is fairly up.'

Even almost entirely non-violent protest might be crushed with extreme force. In the incident which, by far, aroused most controversy within Britain itself, the Jamaican Morant Bay rising of 1865, 354 'rebels' were executed after summary courts martial, at least another 85 killed without even pretence of legal form.

After defeat and occupation, the colonized might continue to reject colonial rule in a great variety of ways. Indeed some historians, seeking to trace these, find anticolonial 'resistance' in almost every kind of action and, for that matter, inaction: from guerrilla war to banditry, from going on strike to working slowly, from verbally abusing whites to evading taxes. The definition of resistance is, surely, being stretched too far. The opposite tendency, that of seeing almost everyone in colonial society as a 'collaborator', is equally unhelpful. It is more fruitful to think of colonial peoples, and most obviously their intellectuals, engaging in a long, complex debate among themselves over how to react to colonialism: a debate which culminated in many of them organizing to overthrow it.

Among the most intense, and among the earliest, stages for these disputes was 19th-century Bengal under British rule. The Bengali intelligentsia rapidly became preoccupied, as Tapan Raychaudhuri says, with 'the anxiety to understand the West, compare her civilization with that of India, discover at least some points where India was equal if not superior to Europe and decide what to adopt and what to reject from the culture of the politically dominant nation'.

Thus the responses to colonialism and to the West of Indian intellectuals were not simply polarized between imitation and rejection, collaboration and resistance. They didn't accept colonialist claims about their own natural inferiority; but nor were they simple-minded enough to believe that 'Europe' was a single homogeneous entity. They knew they could pick and choose among the things British rule and 'European culture' offered them – or sought to impose on them. They accepted some, adapted some to their own purposes, rejected others.

Naturally, this picture cannot be generalized across all colonial situations, or even among Indians outside the educated elite. Certainly the positions of anticolonial intellectuals in Africa and its diaspora were starkly different from that of Bengal. Everywhere there, from colonial Africa itself to the Caribbean, the nationalist intelligentsia was far smaller and more precariously situated than that of India. The comparative lateness of both the colonial impact (1870s–1900s) and the rise of mass nationalism (1940s–1950s) in most of Africa, and the legacy of slavery in the diaspora, complicated their position. Perhaps above all, intellectuals of African descent confronted a European and American cultural contempt which (however invidious such comparisons may be) was undoubtedly more intense and extreme than that faced by Indians. Their reactions to colonial culture were, perhaps, thus more anxious and more polarized than were those in India.

Societies formed largely by the descendants of European settlers and migrants were obviously in a vastly different position. The option of an anticolonial resistance built around assertion of indigenous traditions and resistance to the West was not open, or was so only in drastically modified forms. Postcolonial societies as diverse as Australia, South Africa, and New Zealand are only now, since the late 20th century, really beginning to explore how a common culture can be created, involving elements from both the settlers' descendants and the indigenous peoples.

The situation of the Arab world was different again. Here the direct colonial impact was on the whole later and shorter-lived than in most of Africa, Asia, the Americas, or the Pacific. Over most of south-west Asia direct European, as opposed to Ottoman, domination operated only between the two world wars. Its relatively superficial cultural impact may be gauged by the fact that English and French never seriously challenged Arabic as the main language even of government or literary production. Arab North Africa saw a longer and deeper European penetration. Yet even here, arguably, the colonial presence ushered in less profound social and cultural transformations than in most other parts of the colonized world: except perhaps in Algeria with its huge settler population. In the Arab milieu, the dominant early responses of the intellectuals tended to be of a syncretically 'modernizing' kind. The most profound impact of the West came perhaps *after* the end of formal colonialism. It took forms both wider than European colonialism itself, in the rapid social change which post-war nationalist regimes and swelling oil revenues equally fostered; and narrower, in the specific challenge and affront that the establishment of Israel presented to the Arab world. Largely because of this, confrontation between Westernizing and cultural nationalist schools of thought (the latter ordinarily taking on a specifically religious cast) is fiercer today than it was under European rule.

China's nationalist intellectuals shared with those of the Arab world the position of encountering primarily 'neo-colonial' rather than formal colonial domination. They also shared the situation of reacting to Western dominance from the background of a culture which had for centuries regarded itself, on some legitimate grounds, as intellectually more sophisticated and materially more advanced than those which now penetrated and denigrated it. Beyond such elementary parallels, the story of Chinese reactions to Western incursions cannot be homogenized with any other country or region's experience, any more than can that of Vietnam or Sumatra, Togo or Trinidad, Madagascar or Micronesia. For that matter, there are as many different stories of responses to empire as there were significant thinkers in the European colonies. The pity is that so much recent writing on empire reduces this rich diversity to a

> 'Nationality is an element that springs from the deepest side of men's nature; you can destroy it by severing men from their past . . . But you cannot replace it; for in the isolated shrunken individual, the cut flower of humanity with whom you have now to deal, *you have nothing left to work on.* Such education as you can give him will be the education of a slave: a training not of the whole man, but of certain aptitudes which may render him a useful workman, a pushing tout, or even a prosperous merchant, but never a good citizen. And he will revenge himself on you, in the subtlest and most exasperating of ways, by triumphantly developing into a bad imitation of yourself.
>
> Alfred Zimmern, *Nationality and Government 1918*
> (London, 1918), p. 121, emphasis original.

clutch of formulae and a repetitively recycled handful of supposedly emblematic figures.

Everywhere in the colonial world, cultural assertion had a complex relationship with anticolonialist political nationalism. On the one hand, as had happened earlier in Europe, anticolonial political movements often drew heavily on cultural nationalist ideas. On the other hand, much political nationalism was heavily 'Western' in its formation and outlook. The dominant leaders had mostly been educated in the universities of the colonial powers – or in the USA. They not only sought to establish independent nation-states on a basically European model, but tended also to be – at least rhetorically – modernizing, rationalist, and universalist in their outlook.

This helps explain the persistence and even strengthening of cultural nationalism after political independence. It could be, and was, charged that early nationalist thinkers and post-independence leaders were abjectly Westernized 'mimic men'. They had pursued only political, not economic or cultural, sovereignty. There is thus still almost everywhere in the postcolonial world a vigorous current of cultural criticism devoted to asserting, or recovering, the purity and integrity of indigenous tradition. This sometimes speaks the language of 'racial' character and essence. Although in European contexts such a stance would ordinarily be thought of as adhering to the extreme right in politics, in postcolonial societies it has often been thought of as radical and left-wing; largely because of its association with anti-imperialism. Often, it seemed to involve a simplistic and strident world-view in which everything local and traditional (or supposedly so) was good, everything foreign bad. The great Nigerian writer Wole Soyinka precisely satirized this attitude when he said of the 'judicial' public beating of women in his country's north: 'We need to conserve and display these simple touches of rural elegance in our eternal search and propagation of a national personality.'

Despite this enormous variety of colonial situations, and of responses to them, it has been suggested that one particular kind of colonial encounter stood out from all others: the Muslim one. At the start of the 21st century, and especially since the 11 September 2001 attacks on America by extreme Islamists, it has been widely argued that confrontation between Islamic and Western worlds has its roots in the era of empire.

Yet there may well not have been a sufficiently distinctive Muslim experience of colonialism – or of modernization – to explain anything very much. A century ago, the great majority of the world's Muslims were indeed under European colonial rule: roughly 160 out of 200 million. But so were most Hindus and Buddhists, Sikhs and Jews, and for that matter most non-white Christians and almost all adherents to more localized faiths – the gods of the Yoruba or Kikuyu, Maori or Melanesians. More striking, in comparative perspective, than the colonial subjection of so many Muslims is that a Muslim-ruled, multi-ethnic empire still existed, however enfeebled, under the Ottomans. This is not to say that Muslims under colonial rule had no experiences different from others. I shall hastily sketch a few: but note that none of them applied to all colonized Muslims, nor only to them. And none of them explains nearly as much as other, non-religious variables: differences between British, French, and other systems of rule, between settler and non-settler colonies, between places where colonial rule meant extreme violence and those where it was relatively mild, and so on.

In some – by no means all – colonized Muslim territories, colonial powers were more likely to sustain the positions of indigenous, precolonial rulers, to enlist them as collaborators, and to govern 'through' them, as with the British 'Indirect Rule' philosophy, than in non-Muslim regions. This applied in relation to the Indian princely states (many, but far from all, of whose rulers were Muslim) to West African Emirates (almost all Muslim), and Middle Eastern monarchies and sheikhdoms (invariably Muslim). In Muslim areas, colonial administrators were almost always actively hostile to, or officially forbade, Christian missionary efforts. They were, probably quite rightly, frightened of the reactions which such efforts might provoke. One could thus say that Islamic worship, education, and even legal codes were 'left alone' more than were those of any other religious systems in the colonial world. One consequence in some places was that by the time of independence, Muslim-majority regions lagged substantially behind others in the numbers of Western-educated, widely travelled, or highly qualified personnel they could command. This was starkly the case across much of West Africa, and operated to a lesser but still significant degree in south Asia and parts of the Arab world. Access to certain key skills and opportunities, one could almost say certain key aspects of transnational modernity, was greater, earlier for Hindus (especially West Bengali ones) in the former, members of Christian minorities in the latter, than among Muslims.

For much of the colonial era, there existed in principle – or rather, according to a weak and declining tradition – the idea that Muslims were subject not only to their local rulers, or to the colonialist metropole, but to the Istanbul-based religious authority of the Caliphate. This idea of the Caliphate has, naturally, been important to some modern Islamists. But in the colonial era it was indeed very weak (and was formally abolished in 1924). It didn't prevent Muslims in the British Indian army staying overwhelmingly loyal to the Raj, even against the Turks; nor prevent Arabs from rebelling against their Turkish co-religionists and welcoming 'Christian' aid against them.

Something else, something older, is sometimes claimed to have made Muslim experience of European domination especially wounding. This is that Islamic powers had themselves once been empire builders on a vast scale, unlike any others subjected to colonial rule. This is on one level evidently true, in that no Asante or Inuit could claim or dream that 'their' ancestors had ruled Spain or knocked on the gates of Vienna. But only by a *very* stretched exercise in imagining community and inventing tradition could a Hausa or Kashmiri, a Sudanese or Javanese peasant claim or dream that either. And in fact, unsurprisingly, there seems to be no evidence that they did so. It has also been argued that there existed in the West an especially intense prejudice against the Islamic world, different in kind and greater in virulence than that against other non-Europeans, operating across a broad historical period but persisting into the present. The problem with such a claim is the lack of comparative analysis which might test or validate the claim, measuring Western anti-Islamism against any other kind of prejudice, any other discourse of discrimination, hierarchy, stereotyping, or demonization. For that matter, it is hard to see just how one could quantify different kinds of colonial prejudice in that way, or assign them to a ranking order. Many commentators, moreover, find the entire structure of argument – that 'Islam' and 'the West' form coherent entities, let alone that there is a 'clash of civilizations' between them – intellectually dubious and politically dangerous.

Chapter 4
Ends and aftermaths
of empire

The political decolonization of the European empires took place, with astonishing rapidity, between the end of the Second World War and the 1960s. To say that is, we should immediately note, in a sense misleading. There had been earlier waves of decolonization, as we have seen: the end of European rule in most of the New World in the late 18th and early 19th centuries, and the extension of self-government to Britain's settlement colonies, beginning with Canada in 1839. There were also later ones: Portugal grimly hung on to her African possessions well into the 1970s, the Soviet empire lasted into the 1990s, and British dominion over Hong Kong ended only in 1997. But the wave of accessions to independence in the two decades 1945–65 was without precedent or parallel. Before it, hundreds of millions of people were under European colonial rule; after it, not one tenth as many. Before, only a tiny handful of weak states – China, of course, aside – was ruled by people not of European origin; after, dozens were. Membership of the United Nations more than doubled. Eventually, over a hundred new sovereign states were created. It was one of the most profound transformations the world political system ever experienced. Its only possible rival in importance, during the post-war era, was the Cold War. To many, it marked the end not just of formal colonial rule, but of the era of European dominance, and of the very idea of empire.

It was, in the main, a remarkably non-violent process. True, there were numerous, bitter wars of decolonization. They were as various as the local experiences of decolonization itself. They included, for France, Vietnam 1946–54, Morocco 1952–6, Algeria 1954–62, Cameroon 1955–8, plus – more massacre than war – Madagascar 1947–8. For Britain, Palestine, Malaya, Kenya, Cyprus, Aden, and maybe – a marginal case since Britain was not, officially, defending its own sovereign territory – the conflict in Borneo in 1964–5. But, contrary to much anticolonial nationalist rhetoric, they were *not* the typical experience of decolonization. British disengagements from empire, especially, were in most cases largely consensual. They might involve strikes, riots, the almost ritual imprisonment of nationalist leaders – being a 'prison graduate' was a near-obligatory credential for popular legitimacy, and Ghanaian politicians campaigned for election in little white caps embossed 'PG'. But they did not usually involve war. When they did, it was because one or more of three factors was in play, blocking consensual decolonization: the presence of white settler minorities, strategic importance of the colony to the metropole, nationalist movements adopting an unusually radical or pro-Communist ideology.

The armed conflicts which did occur were mostly small wars at least on the colonizers' side. In the British case, they were also strikingly uncontentious within domestic politics. Both physical and, even more, psychological distance told against British opinion becoming as intensely engaged or divided by colonial war as did the French over Algeria. The only British colony as important to Britain as Algeria was to France – economically, militarily, emotionally – was India. Once it was gone, decolonization lost a significant part of its psychic charge. Britain's colonial wars were all far away. The enemies were not, with the partial exception of the Zionist movement, ones with whom many people in Britain had an intense fellow feeling or close prior links.

Divisions in France over colonial conflicts were of course

15. Resisters: 'The Sniper', an Afridi warrior on the Khyber Pass, North-West Frontier of British India, c.1920. This individual is not as deadly as he looks – his elderly musket appears to be broken. But men like him, on the frontier and across it in Afghanistan, repeatedly defied British rule for a century, and afterwards proved a menace to post-independence governments and Russian invaders too.

considerably sharper, especially as the Algerian war escalated. France's assimilationist and centralizing colonial ethos had perhaps a stronger emotional appeal to the general public than Britain's traditions of aristocratic empire, 'Indirect Rule', and decentralization had to the average post-war British voter. In a word, the official French presentation of its colonial mission was more modernizing than Britain's. It was, or had become, Republican rather than aristocratic. And French racial discourse was, on the face of it, more benignly paternalist than British; centred on culture rather than biology. In a less forward-looking spirit, important interest groups within France – not least in the military – saw retention of empire and victory in colonial wars as a compensation for the humiliations of defeat by Germany in 1940. Finally, much French opinion saw decolonization as tied to the economic or even demographic survival of France herself; to an extent unthinkable in the more self-confident, or complacent, post-war British political culture.

Britain's political system, then, was largely unshaken by the end of empire. Although decolonization was accompanied by widespread lamentations at national decline, these were usually expressed in tones of wistful regret, not panic or anger. France, in stark contrast, had its political institutions torn apart by the colonial war in Algeria and its end – though recovery thereafter was remarkably quick. For Portugal, a little later, decolonization seemed a positive boon. It both enabled, and was enabled by, the internal transition from dictatorship to democracy, which in turn made possible the country's entry into the European mainstream, and the European Union. The experiences of the smaller imperial powers – notably Belgium and Holland – fell somewhere in between. Both were briefly wracked with anguish over the loss of their colonies, but both then appeared rapidly to sublimate the experience and turn enthusiastically to Europeanization instead: though the machinations of Belgian officials and mining companies in their former central African fiefdoms later returned to haunt the Brussels scene.

It would be impossible here to summarize the multiple lines of argument that have been advanced to explain the causes, timing, and character of decolonization. Some are complementary, others sharply conflicting. But David Abernethy is surely correct to say that the single most decisive factor was not a change in colonized people's *capacity* to challenge imperial rule, but an increased – or more widespread – *will* to do so. This was significantly prompted by developments within Europe. The spread of both democratic and nationalist ideas there encouraged colonial elites to believe that they could, and should, emulate those transformations – and that the continuation of colonial rule was increasingly incompatible with the Europeans' own proclaimed values. More immediately powerful, though, were developments within colonial society. The coalitions of local support, or acquiescence, on which imperial rule depended began to unravel under pressure from a range of forces, including the more interventionist policies which most colonial governments themselves sponsored in their last years. New political movements, led by anticolonial nationalists, began to build their own, rival coalitions – though post-independence developments in many countries showed these often to be very fragile. Those nationalist elites, and the most important sections of their early followers, were themselves products of colonial modernity. Colonialism was thus a self-defeating enterprise, in that it introduced – however slowly and grudgingly – into its possessions both the ideas and the social forces which were to bring it down.

Many other developments were also in play. One could point to the new 'bargains' struck between nationalist elites and outgoing colonial rulers, aimed primarily at pre-empting mass unrest; to the vastly increased cost of holding down a rebellious population under modern economic and military conditions; the 'demonstration effect' of successful nationalist struggles elsewhere; the role of financial interests, of international public opinion, and of the Cold War. All of these combined to convince the more far-sighted colonial powers that they could not afford indefinitely to repress

16. Collaborators: Armed black South African police during the 1976 Soweto uprising. The apartheid regime was often described as one of 'internal colonialism'. Like almost all earlier colonial systems, its rule depended on recruiting black as well as white auxiliaries.

nationalism: they had to co-opt, cultivate, or create amenable successors who could be counted on to preserve the more essential interests of the metropole. Such successors were not ordinarily to be found among the 'traditional rulers' or 'martial races' who had been the main collaborators or subcontractors of empire – though in a few cases power was transferred to them. They lay rather in an often small but fast-growing indigenous middle class: more often professional than commercial or industrial. A very high proportion of the successful nationalist challengers were lawyers, while their lower-ranking local lieutenants were often teachers and journalists. A remarkable number were also poets, though rarely very good ones. It was very much the same social profile that had characterized Irish, Czech, or Serbian nationalist movements a few generations earlier.

When they acceded to power, these men (there were almost no women among them) faced immense difficulties – which were perhaps at their greatest in much of sub-Saharan Africa. They had inherited states, but few of them were nations in the 19th-century European understanding, in that they had little historical, cultural, or linguistic unity. Their boundaries were mostly products of late-Victorian negotiation between colonial powers, bearing no relation to precolonial political or ethnic entities. They often lumped together many diverse groups, and divided some previously more cohesive ones. In many cases, the only common language was that of the former colonial power – command of which was restricted to those same elites. The task of nation-building was only made more strenuous by the facts that so many of these new states were very poor, dangerously dependent on a single agricultural or mineral export or on foreign loans (with, eventually, crippling consequent burdens of debt), and lacking in established democratic institutions. It remains intensely controversial how much all this should be 'blamed' on the legacy of colonialism; though it must be added that many of the new rulers – or the military governments which often rapidly replaced them – proved to be inept, corrupt, or dictatorial.

The ensuing conflicts and instability in much of postcolonial Africa, the Arab world, and parts of Asia are often referred to as stemming from 'tribalism'. But many historians argue that we cannot explain political conflict as a product of 'tribal' antagonisms, when the tribal identities concerned are often themselves products of the conflicts. Analysts of Africa's worst postcolonial disaster, the 1990s genocide in Rwanda, pointed out that there were hardly any real cultural distinctions between the 'ethnic groups' in conflict, Hutu and Tutsi – and certainly no important physical differences, despite the myth-making of colonial ethnography. The idea of rigidly defined and fiercely opposed Tutsi and Hutu identities, it was suggested, was largely a creation of colonial policies, and was then sustained and manipulated by rival post-independence politicians for their own narrow ends.

Some visionaries believed, in the years immediately before and after independence, that the only solution to such massive problems lay in far wider unifying or federal structures: African unity, pan-Arab federation, and so on. In Africa the Ghanaian leader Kwame Nkrumah, though a spectacularly unsuccessful ruler in his own country, remained widely revered as the protagonist of such a continent-wide vision. Egyptian President Gamal Abdul Nasser was a similarly inspiring exponent of unity to many Arabs. Some urged, and sought to build, still broader solidarities, encompassing the entire postcolonial world. The great symbolic moment of aspiration was the 1955 Bandung conference, bringing together 29 leaders of new African and Asian countries in ringing declarations of cooperation and common destiny. It was hoped in some quarters that such developments heralded a general move forward from a localized and reactive anticolonial nationalism to a far more universal 'liberationist' stage. The politics of liberation would go beyond nationalism to unite all of the postcolonial 'wretched of the earth': one which, in some formulations, would involve not only political freedom but also economic justice, the rights of women, and much more. Perhaps the most eloquent exponent of such a vision was the Martiniquan writer Frantz Fanon.

17. **Resisters:** Born in French-ruled Martinique, the psychologist and anticolonial theorist Frantz Fanon, who spent his last years working for the Algerian revolution against France, was perhaps the most powerfully articulate advocate of decolonization as heralding a totally new and better era for humanity. Yet he is also – perhaps rather unfairly – remembered for his belief in the liberating nature of violence.

Such dreams of universal postcolonial liberation have never entirely vanished. But in many places, a quite opposite story came to be told: one of lapse or decline from an inclusive and generously conceived liberatory nationalism into a narrower, more sectarian postcolonial politics of ethnic, communal, 'tribal', or religious antagonisms. This has, for instance, been a characteristic view among modern Indian writers who see late-colonial and postcolonial bigotry or violence, especially between Hindus and Muslims, as a degenerate offshoot of nationalist politics. Communalism was nationalism gone wrong.

The institutions projected or created by figures like Nkrumah and Nasser, or at events like Bandung, meanwhile either failed to take off or persisted only in enfeebled, widely discredited form. The Non-Aligned Movement which grew from Bandung soon fell captive to Cold War antagonisms; the Organization of African Unity became notable mainly for the costly ostentation of its summit meetings, and for its persistent failure even to debate, let alone act on, the crimes of some of Africa's leaders. Perhaps ironically, international associations formed by the former colonial powers sometimes had more durability. France retained very strong economic, political, cultural, and, in emergencies, military links with many of her former colonies, especially in Africa. 'Francafrique' remained a real entity, and in critics' eyes a direct continuation of colonialism. The shadowy Jacques Foccart, adviser on African affairs to successive French presidents, probably wielded more real power on the continent than almost any of its countries' own leaders. Perhaps more hopeful was the main institutional legatee of the British empire, the Commonwealth. Though seen by its critics as little more than an imperial hangover, and although it is a looser (and certainly a less British-dominated) association than its early architects had expected, it has successfully refashioned itself into a modest but positive example of internationalism, especially valuable to its smaller and poorer members. Friendship, democracy, or social justice were far from universal among its members; but as a group, their average standards of democratic governance and

113

human rights observance were clearly higher than those of the postcolonial world as a whole. One indicator of relative success was that, in the 1990s, several postcolonial states which had never been parts of Britain's empire sought to join.

New empires for old?

The age of formal empire is clearly dead. Direct physical control of territories outside one's own has long been almost invariably a financial burden rather than an asset. It is certain that not one of the remaining scattered British or French colonies brings in a profit to the owner's exchequer. Equally, maintaining client states – the main mode of informal empire in the modern world – also seems usually to be an expensive business. Not even the bitterest critic of American policy in Vietnam, the Philippines, or Afghanistan would suggest that the US Treasury returned a profit on the deals. The Soviet Union's junior partners in Eastern Europe, still more in Cuba and Africa, were subsidized from Moscow; not vice versa. Ever since the Second World War, the trend was towards new and less direct ways of exerting influence. The problem for great powers was that the repertoire of such means has always been rather limited, and all of them can get one involved in disastrous entanglements. The most obvious, and in the abstract perhaps least objectionable, kind of informal *imperium* is that exercised by a country seeking to protect its interests and those of its friends by taking on a 'policing' role in regional conflicts. Both superpowers, in pursuit of this strategy, experienced numerous spectacular failures through the 1970s and 1980s. The US and its allies' apparently successful intervention in the Gulf in 1990–1 was almost the only, though problematic, exception to the picture. But it appeared to set a pattern for the future, for thereafter direct military intervention – sometimes by the USA acting alone, sometimes under the auspices of NATO, sometimes of the United Nations – increased in frequency, and perhaps in effectiveness.

Only a very strong, perhaps only a globally dominant, power can

18. The debris of a lost colonial war: wrecked Soviet tank in Afghanistan, 1980s.

sustain informal empire in the long run. Direct political rule requires a range of at least minimally competent, trustworthy local allies. The exercise of indirect domination needs them even more, and needs more of them: one must work through people with some claim to local legitimacy. One needs, bluntly, to be able to buy such people, offering direct subsidies, or links of trade, aid, and investment, that will woo them to one's side, or access to cultural capital that confers local prestige (as deployed with some success by the French in their former colonies), or at the very least the weapons that will keep them in power when all else fails. In the Cold War era, the USA could offer all these, and still fail to maintain stable spheres of influence. The Soviets could provide only the last. No wonder they were never very successful imperialists, and were ordinarily cautious enough to avoid major direct commitments beyond the spheres of influence allotted them at Yalta.

The world after the Cold War is clearly different in all those respects; but it is still too soon really to say *how* different – let alone what effect the dramatic developments since September 2001 will have. On a global scale, only one country could now even dream of maintaining an informal empire. And it is of course immensely contentious whether the power and policies of the United States represent either the fact of such an empire, or an aspiration towards it. At the moment of writing, the USA's global power is so great, so lacking in serious rivals, that it considerably outstrips that exercised by Britain at its 19th-century peak of influence. Some would say that the closest parallel is with imperial Rome at the time when it entirely dominated what was then known as the world.

It has indeed been suggested that such a comparison can be extended considerably further. As with ancient Rome, so today, 'empire' is seen by most of those who live within it as synonymous with the civilized – though today they might more often say, the democratic – world. Outside are barbarians who, if they attack or reject the empire, can be motivated only by envy, bitterness, refusal to accept the obvious superiority of its values. And those values are superior not for any ethnocentric or nationalistic reason. On the contrary, their greatness lies in their universality. The new idea of empire is like the ancient Roman and medieval Christian ones, unlike the imperial systems that rose and fell in between, in that it is, or aspires to be, a *universal* order. The United States, with its close allies, is the only force that can maintain global peace and justice – if necessary, by force – not in pursuit of a nationalist or a power-hungry agenda, but to uphold those universal values.

Such an argument surely pushes too far. It probably, and simply, makes the United States sound more powerful than it really is. It underestimates the actual or potential tensions between universalism and narrower national interests in American thought, those between globalism and isolationism in US foreign policy, and those between the USA and even its most faithful allies like Britain. It makes it sound as though all the different interests involved in America's influence on the world – multinational companies, cultural institutions, the government, and the armed forces – form a monolith, with a shared aim and world-view. US military intervention in postcolonial countries, and the global spread of McDonald's restaurants, might both be seen by those who dislike them as forms of empire-building; but they are hardly the same thing as one another.

The idea of a new, universal world empire makes too much of the supposed novelty of a single global order, without significant challenges or rivalries. In that, it echoes some of the more overblown claims of current 'globalization theory'. Actually, as we noted above, there have been major elements of a worldwide system of economic – and cultural – exchange in existence for a long time, many of them the creations of older empires. And today, there is not a single seamless web, but regional economic blocs – Europe and Japan as well as America – whose interests may conflict, while individual states other than the USA, even poor postcolonial ones, still have more power than such a picture suggests.

19–22. **Imperialists?** Four candidates for the title of 'last great empire-builder'. Nazi leader Heinrich Himmler briefly ruled a vast slave empire in Eastern Europe and planned a racist utopia of perpetual 'Aryan' dominion there. US President Harry S. Truman put in place the post-war doctrine that America could intervene anywhere in the world that its interests were threatened. Soviet President Leonid Brezhnev initiated the disastrous Russian intervention in Afghanistan, and presided over the economic decay of the USSR itself. And 'Ronald McDonald', the clown used for promotional purposes by McDonald's burger chain, sold an identically tasteless product right round the globe.

And the notion that a single set of cultural forms and values
dominates the globe, or tries to do so, is also too simple. Not
everything courses out from the centre. There was no ancient
Roman equivalent – indeed no real parallel before today – for the
multi-directionality, as well as the scale, of modern flows of
information, people, ideas, cultural forms. Theories of neo-
colonialism and cultural imperialism often understate the
complexity and multifariousness of postcolonial cultural travellings.
To take just one example, the Congo (former Zaire) is today perhaps
the world's most spectacular example of a 'failed state'. Even before
its collapse, it endured decades of corrupt dictatorship and ever-
deepening poverty. Before *that* was civil war, and before that again
one of the most brutal and devastating of all colonial experiences.
A vast, thinly populated country of immense ethnic diversity, it
possessed no cohesive cultural traditions; while its erstwhile
Belgian rulers said, naturally, that it had no culture worth the
name at all.

Against that miserable background, the pan-African and global
reach of Congolese music is an utterly unexpected phenomenon. Its
performers were much influenced by new musical styles from the
other side of the Atlantic, especially Cuban ones: but these in their
turn had been heavily shaped by more distant African sources. A
kind of 'repatriation' was thus involved, but a very complex,
indirect, and mediated kind. It uses mostly electric instruments, but
draws heavily on indigenous styles and themes. Congolese artists
like Franco Luambo Makiadi – the most popular and influential of
all – became their country's cultural ambassadors, and its unofficial
poets laureate. Their lyrics reflected every aspect of the society's
concerns, but also underlined how transnational these were: Franco
sang the praises of Volkswagen cars as well as of the local dictator
(he was, of course, paid to do both), warned against both witchcraft
and AIDS. Congolese music achieved its own kind of 'cultural
imperialism', spreading and being copied almost throughout Africa
– to the loud displeasure of cultural nationalists in many other
countries – and beyond. But, in a further ironic twist, the centres of

23. **Globalizing African culture after empire: Franco Luambo Makiadi, Congolese singer and bandleader.**

recording, marketing, and distribution for this music are not in central Africa itself, but in the former imperial capitals of Brussels and Paris. In spheres like music, sport, popular fiction, even TV soap opera, the postcolonial story is not just one of Euro-American dominance, nor of 'nativist' cultural resistance, but an immensely rich, complex nexus of appropriation, adaptation, indigenization – and of influences flowing from Kinshasa to Brussels, Bombay to London, Havana to New York.

Chapter 5
Studying and judging empires

We are now, maybe, just distant enough from the multiple decolonizations of the 20th century to begin to see them in properly historical, and comparative, perspective. We can try, with more clarity than was possible before, to judge what was distinctive about European empire-building. Why did the states of Western Europe – first Spain and Portugal, then the British, Dutch, and French – rise to global dominance? What made their expansion different from, and so much more far-reaching than, the creation of continental empires by Austria, Prussia, and Russia, or by the Arabs, Turks, and Chinese? Why did these Western European empires, far more than any others in history, succeed in transforming almost everything right across the world, from political systems to ecologies? Why did such empires persist into the mid-20th century, and why did they eventually collapse with such remarkable speed? We may even be able, by now, to attempt some kind of ethical judgement about empire, a balance sheet of its crimes and its achievements. Were the European colonial systems, on balance, destructive or creative forces?

Historians have taken the rise and fall of empires as one of their great themes ever since there has been such a thing as historical writing. Most ancient Greek and Roman chroniclers wrote, in a sense, imperial history. Probably the most famous and widely read pre-modern historical work in English is Edward Gibbon's *Decline and Fall of the Roman Empire*. In more recent times, ideas about imperialism and colonialism have become crucial, apparently almost ubiquitous, themes in almost every field of academic and cultural debate: most obviously now in literary and cultural studies, but also in political theory, economics and 'development studies', anthropology, theology, and of course history. And they have done so carrying a weighty conceptual and political baggage, including, at the present moment, a major influence from postmodernist and poststructuralist theory. They have intertwined – sometimes productively, often explosively – with issues of nationalism, community, and ethnicity, of gender, class, and perhaps above all those of 'race'. In some hands, the idea of empire has come to be seen as synonymous with modernity itself. At every step, these enormously varied attempts to study, and sometimes to judge, the history of empires have posed questions of the relationships among knowledge, identity, and power.

In recent years the greatest focus of attention has been on cultural studies of empire, looking at the imagery, literary representations, beliefs, and ideologies which empire builders, and their opponents, produced. Some historians argue that there has been too much concentration on these subjects, which may not be quite so important as they are often now thought to be. Imperial ideologies, such critics suggest, were often just window-dressing, rationalizations for acts of conquest and forms of rule which were actually driven by quite different forces. Expansion was perhaps often opportunistic, improvised, or a response to crisis, rather than motivated by grand ideologies or powerful cultural forces. Understanding empire may sometimes be furthered more by looking at its *means* – notably the technological inequalities, especially in military hardware, which for a time made it comparatively easy, cheap, and risk-free for some societies to dominate others – than by investigation of culture and ideology. There was, on this view, rarely a grand plan for empire.

We might also, some warn, be wary of overstating the power of empire. A substantial body of recent writing has stressed how dramatically and totally colonial rulers reshaped the societies they dominated. This included the widespread 'invention of tradition' there: for instance, it is suggested, Indian ideas of 'caste' and African ones of 'tribe' were entirely transformed if not simply fabricated by colonialism. Such views, however, might greatly overestimate the inventive capacity of European rulers and understate that of their subjects. They might make colonialism sound too much like a single, conscious, cohesive, and all-powerful entity. And they might tend to ignore or downplay important continuities between precolonial and colonial history – and indeed between colonial and postcolonial times too.

This is not to deny that, in some circumstances, the colonial impact was literally catastrophic and even genocidal. This is most evidently the case with those settler-colonial conquests, in parts of the Americas and Australasia, where indigenous peoples were reduced to a fraction of their former numbers or even disappeared altogether under the onslaught of dispossession, disease, and massacre. But there were other episodes of utter destruction which have been almost entirely forgotten, like the disappearance of the Guanche people of the Canary islands under the European impact. Few, if any, modern tourists in the islands are likely to be aware that they are visiting a place that was once the site of mass murder. Still today, there are small indigenous peoples in the Amazon basin and in Antarctica which are threatened with total extinction. Most historians are sceptical about whether the European conquerors really *intended* the complete elimination of those they conquered. Some would therefore doubt whether words like genocide are really appropriate. But that was the undoubted *effect* of European actions in some places.

Even in Africa, where the direct colonial impact was generally later, more short-lived and, so many analysts would concur, more superficial than in most other parts of the colonial world, there were instances of populational and/or cultural collapse. Thus in German

South-West Africa (now Namibia), the Nama and Herero people were subjected to a deliberate, and largely successful, military campaign of mass extermination. And the extreme physical repression and scorn for 'native' life pursued in the rainforests of Equatorial Africa by French, German, and especially Belgian occupiers resulted, in the view of the region's most distinguished historian, Jan Vansina, in the almost complete breakdown of indigenous tradition. This was 'an apocalyptic conquest', which killed approximately half the area's total population and left the remainder as 'cultural schizophrenics . . . bereft of a common mind and purpose'. Vansina's, though, is an unusually stark view of an unusually traumatic colonizing process. In general, colonial conquest was nearly always partial, the processes of social and cultural change it sponsored or unleashed still more so. The ideologies of colonial expansion and rule, too, were far more varied and ambiguous than is routinely suggested in much current writing. To recognize and explore this is not to 'rehabilitate' the colonial record, nor to excuse or downplay the violence, oppression, and exploitation that marked almost all its passages.

The modern emphasis on the cultures of colonialism may also sometimes lead to relative neglect of economic and political forces. In many ways empire was very specifically a political phenomenon, a matter of the state. A key part of what defines it, I have suggested, is the way in which the colonizing state took complete power over the government of the territory which it had annexed. This clearly distinguishes colonial polities from those which have internal self-government, such as British Dominions, and from formally sovereign states subject to various forms and degrees of influence or control from outside (though the latter, by the definitions we have adopted, may well be instances of *imperialism*). We should, this implies, be giving more attention to the political and legal systems of empires, and their rulers' ideas about law and order. It is important to see how interest groups, religious bodies, business firms, educational institutions, and so on acted under colonial conditions, but this must include thinking about their relationships to colonial state power. Part of this is a need always to ask ourselves: what was *different* about religion, education, law, economic activity, and all the other spheres of life under colonialism? What, if anything, did all the immensely varied colonial situations have in common which marked them out from others? Might it even be that on a wider and longer-term view, looking at interactions between human groups across the sweep of history, then we might see cultural interchange, export, and expansion as more important than empire? We might even see colonialism itself, in any strict or coherent sense, as a mere effect of all those processes of cultural diffusion, export, copying, fusion, mongrelization or interaction. Some historians suggest that the most important consequence of empire was the way it spread originally European state systems and economic patterns to cover the world. But others think most of this would have happened anyway, with or without colonial rule. Japan, to take the most obvious and most successful example, was never colonized, but still effectively copied those systems and patterns.

Arguments over how *important* empires were in human history are not at all the same as *moral* evaluations of their records and legacies – though some influential writers do seem to confuse the two. Most historians, meanwhile, feel uncomfortable with explicit moral judgements: but may nonetheless often smuggle them in undercover. The modern consensus view is to judge the legacies of empire, especially of the modern European empires, very harshly. The racism which usually suffused them, and their assaults on their subjects' human dignity and self-esteem, are held especially guilty. Empire, moreover, is seen as inherently incompatible with democracy, and of course with self-determination.

There are arguments the other way. We have seen that a case can be made for seeing modern empire as economically progressive, and generally beneficial even to the colonized. Politically too, it can be proposed that at least some great modern empires – the British,

French, Austro-Hungarian, Russian, and even the Ottoman – had virtues that have been too readily forgotten. They provided stability, security, and legal order for their subjects. They constrained, and at their best tried to transcend, the potentially savage ethnic or religious antagonisms among their peoples. And the aristocracies which ruled most of them were often far more liberal, humane, and cosmopolitan than their supposedly more democratic successors. The rivers of blood undammed by each empire's fall, from the partition of India to the current fate of Chechnya, should make us think again about the alleged virtues of 'national democracy', in whose name so much atrocity is sanctified.

Transcending or sidestepping such emotionally charged arguments, some historians would now want to ask: 'What was so special about Europe anyway?' The idea of fundamental, absolute differences between 'East' and 'West', Europe and the rest, has been one of the most constantly renewed clichés of world history. It is, some think, at least as old as the Greek–Persian wars of 2,500 years ago – and as new as febrile current debates about the 'clash of civilizations'. Yet the argument has perpetually changed its form, and the boundary between Us and Them has been unendingly fluid. It has never been clear where Europe ends and Asia starts, geographically or culturally. In one sense, that's what Greeks and Turks, Serbs and Croats, even Russian presidential candidates, fight each other about. The dominant approach has been to start from the assumption of Europe's uniqueness – above all, as sole birthplace of capitalism – and then seek to explain it. A long tradition, unfortunately by no means defunct, used the categories of race to account for divergent historical paths. Nowadays, the concept of cultural difference, just as all-embracing and almost as meaningless as race once was, is employed to the same ends.

That still powerful picture has had to undergo a whole series of ad hoc adjustments. First Japan's rise had to be fitted to it. This was usually done by arguing that it was possible because Japan, uniquely in Asia, had a European-style feudal tradition, or a successful 'bourgeois revolution', or entrepreneurial cultural values, or because it was never under colonial rule. But as country after country in east Asia moved into economic take-off, the original assumption became ever harder to sustain: too many exceptions disproved the rule. We must, some suggest, take a much longer historical view, which reveals that the differences which are supposed to have determined European economic dynamism and Asian stagnation either don't exist, or can't explain what they are alleged to. It is not true that Europe developed unique forms of rationality, of business enterprise, of individualism, or attitudes to work or property: or not true enough to mark out an essential East–West division. Even something as mundane but crucial to the emergence of capitalism, and supposedly distinctive to Western Europe, as double-entry bookkeeping has close parallels in medieval India, China, and Egypt. Reasons for global success or failure must be far more contingent than has been thought.

Finally, some important trends in the world of the early 21st century give the history of empires a renewed relevance, and enable new perspectives on it. Globalization today underlines the value of thinking about the global systems of the past. Historians during the 20th century tended overwhelmingly to write about single countries – almost always their own. Outside the academic world, popular historical consciousness and the teaching of history in schools was, and still is, almost entirely national – and indeed national*ist* – in focus. Among the very first actions of most postcolonial states, on or even before achieving their independence, was to revive or create 'national histories' like the European ones. Today, it is increasingly widely recognized that historical understanding, if it is kept within those narrow national boundaries, will not equip the citizens of the 21st century anywhere on earth to understand their world. They may, or may not, be citizens of a new world empire – perhaps an economic, cultural, or media empire, if not a political one. They may even be barbarians, outcasts, or refugees knocking vainly at the gates of such an empire.

But they will be world citizens, more fully than their ancestors ever were. To understand what that means, they will need to know something about the global empires of the past.

References

Chapter 1

Jeffrey Jerome Cohen (ed.), *The Postcolonial Middle Ages* (London, 2000)

Elleke Boehmer, *Colonial and Postcolonial Literature* (Oxford, 1995), p. 1

Charles W. Mills, *The Racial Contract* (Ithaca, NY, 1997)

David Cannadine, *Ornamentalism* (London 2001)

Chapter 3

Gauri Viswanathan, *Masks of Conquest* (New York, 1989); Samuel, *Theatres of Memory* (London, 1994) p. 232

Johannes Fabian, *Out of Our Minds: Reason and Madness in the Exploration of Central Africa* (Berkeley, 2000)

Estimate (p. 5) from Mahir Saul and Patrick Royer, *West African Challenge to Empire* (Athens and Oxford, 2001)

Quotation from T. O. Ranger, *Revolt in Southern Rhodesia 1896–7* (London, 1967), p. 131

Tapan Raychaudhuri, *Europe Reconsidered* (Delhi, 1988), p. 333

Wole Soyinka: quoted in James Gibbs and Bernth Lindfors, *Research on Wole Soyinka* (Trenton, NJ, 1993), p. 239

Chapter 5

Jan Vansina, *Paths in the Rainforests* (London, 1990), p. 239

Further reading

Perhaps the most stimulating recent overview of ancient empires, comparing them with more modern ones, is Susan E. Alcock and others (eds.), *Empires* (Cambridge, 2001). A little older, and only available in French, but extremely valuable, is Maurice Duverger (ed.), *Le Concept d'Empire* (Paris, 1980). On the Chinese empires, one might start with J. K. Fairbank, *China: A New History* (Cambridge, Mass., 1992), while Thomas J. Barfield, *The Perilous Frontier: Nomadic Empires and China* (Oxford, 1992) tackles one of the most neglected parts of this vast field. For Muslim empire-building – and universalism – Marshall Hodgson, *The Venture of Islam* (3 vols., Chicago, 1974) remains a classic, though unwieldy and contentious, study.

Challenges to historians' Eurocentrism have, happily, proliferated in recent years. Among those most relevant to the comparative study of empires are Janet Abu-Lughod, *Before European Hegemony: The World System, 1250–1350* (Oxford, 1989) and K. N. Chaudhuri, *Asia Before Europe: Economy and Civilization of the Indian Ocean from the Rise of Islam to c.1750* (Cambridge, 1990). The most influential exposition of ideas about historical 'world systems' and 'world empires', Immanuel Wallerstein, *The Modern World System* (3 vols., New York, 1974, 1980, and 1989) is still somewhat more Europe-centred.

Among overviews of modern empires, David B. Abernethy, *The Dynamics of Global Dominance* (New Haven and London, 2000), is the widest-ranging, Jurgen Osterhammel, *Colonialism* (Princeton, 1997) the most systematic and succinct, Anthony Pagden, *Peoples and Empires* (London, 2001) – which especially stresses the links between empire-building and mass migration – perhaps the most vividly written. Dominic Lieven, *Empire: The Russian Empire and its Rivals* (London, 2000) is, as the subtitle suggests, strongest on Russian expansion and decline, but makes important comparative arguments too. More theoretical, sometimes ponderous, but important are such social-scientific works as Michael Doyle, *Empires* (Ithaca, NY, and London, 1986) and Alexander J. Motyl, *Imperial Ends: The Decay, Collapse, and Revival of Empires* (New York, 2001).

The works of Edward W. Said have been far the most influential and controversial cultural studies of empire, especially *Orientalism* (London and New York, 1978) and *Culture and Imperialism* (London and New York, 1993). Among the many 'anti-Saidian' works produced in response, perhaps the most interesting for historians are John MacKenzie, *Orientalism: History, Theory and the Arts* (Manchester, 1995) and David Cannadine, *Ornamentalism: How the British Saw their Empire* (London, 2001). The colonial and postcolonial studies 'industry' has spawned a vast number of anthologies and introductory texts aimed mainly at students, but probably the best, certainly the widest-ranging, is Robert J. C. Young, *Postcolonialism* (Oxford, 2001). A kind of counterpoint to Young's book, with a more conservative political stance and a greater emphasis on economics, is D. K. Fieldhouse, *The West and the Third World* (Oxford 1999).

Elleke Boehmer (ed.), *Empire Writing* (Oxford, 1998) gives a taste of the many kinds of pro- and anti-imperial literature in English. In the long tradition of writing against empire, perhaps the most lastingly resonant texts have proved to be J. A. Hobson, *Imperialism* (London, 1902) and Frantz Fanon, *The Wretched of the Earth* (originally in French 1961, English edn. London, 1965).

The Oxford History of the British Empire (general ed. Wm Roger Louis, Oxford 1998–9) is extremely uneven in scope and quality – as a project with five large volumes and dozens of authors is bound to be – but the best parts are very good indeed. If you want a much shorter overview of British imperialism, but still one reflecting a diversity of viewpoints, P. J. Marshall (ed.), *The Cambridge Illustrated History of the British Empire* (Cambridge, 1996) is a good bet. The most-debated single recent viewpoint, by contrast, is P. J. Cain and A. G. Hopkins, *British Imperialism* (2 vols., London, 1993; 2nd. edn. 2001).

On the relationship between the history of empire and current debates on globalization, A. G. Hopkins (ed.), *Globalization in World History* (London, 2002) is a pioneering collection, which will surely soon spawn many imitators. Michael Hardt and Antonio Negri, *Empire* (Cambridge, Mass., 2000) is one of the most debated visions of the 'imperial' present and future.

Index

Expand your collection of
VERY SHORT INTRODUCTIONS